The History

From Kilimanjaro

to Zanzibar

The Land of Kilimanjaro: Tanzania's Geographical Marvels

Tanzania, a country located in East Africa, is blessed with a diverse and awe-inspiring geography that has captivated explorers, adventurers, and nature enthusiasts for centuries. One of its most iconic and majestic features is Mount Kilimanjaro, Africa's tallest mountain and a symbol of Tanzania's natural splendor.

Rising to an astonishing height of 5,895 meters (19,341 feet), Mount Kilimanjaro stands proudly as the highest freestanding mountain in the world. Its distinctive snow-capped peak, known as Kibo, is a sight to behold and has enticed countless climbers to conquer its formidable slopes. Kilimanjaro's three volcanic cones, namely Kibo, Mawenzi, and Shira, form a breathtaking landscape that is both imposing and ethereal.

The mountain is situated in the northeastern part of Tanzania, near the border with Kenya. Its location within the Kilimanjaro National Park adds to its allure, as the park encompasses a vast area of approximately 1,688 square kilometers (652 square miles) and protects a rich tapestry of ecosystems. From lush rainforests to alpine meadows and barren volcanic terrain, Kilimanjaro National Park offers a remarkable variety of habitats, each harboring its own unique flora and fauna.

The slopes of Mount Kilimanjaro provide a haven for a diverse range of plant and animal species. As climbers ascend the mountain, they pass through distinct ecological zones characterized by varying vegetation. The lower slopes are adorned with dense rainforests teeming with life, including a myriad of bird species, colorful butterflies, and small mammals such as the elusive tree hyrax. Towering trees, such as camphor and fig, dominate the landscape, providing shelter and sustenance to a thriving ecosystem.

As the altitude increases, the rainforest gives way to a belt of moorland characterized by heath-like vegetation, scattered tussock grass, and an abundance of unique plant species adapted to the harsh alpine conditions. Giant lobelias and groundsel plants dot the landscape, lending an otherworldly charm to the surroundings. Here, visitors may spot the occasional hyrax or high-altitude bird species soaring above.

Continuing further up the mountain, the landscape transforms into an alpine desert, with rocky expanses devoid of vegetation. The air becomes thin, and the temperatures drop drastically, testing the endurance of climbers who brave the summit push. Yet, even in this seemingly inhospitable environment, life persists in the form of resilient mosses, lichens, and hardy alpine flowers that manage to eke out an existence amidst the challenging conditions.

The summit of Mount Kilimanjaro is a sight that leaves an indelible mark on all who reach its pinnacle. At Uhuru Peak, the highest point on the mountain, climbers are rewarded with sweeping panoramic views that stretch across the vast expanse of the African plains. On a clear day, one can gaze upon the distant Serengeti, the Ngorongoro Crater, and even catch a glimpse of the shimmering waters of Lake Victoria.

Beyond Mount Kilimanjaro, Tanzania boasts a wealth of geographical marvels that contribute to its extraordinary diversity. To the north, the country is bordered by the expansive Lake Victoria, the largest freshwater lake in Africa and the second-largest freshwater lake in the world. Its shores are a hive of activity, supporting thriving fishing communities and serving as a vital water source for the surrounding regions.

Towards the west, Tanzania is home to Lake Tanganyika, the longest freshwater lake in the world and an ecological treasure trove. Its crystal-clear waters harbor an incredible array of fish species, many of which are found nowhere else on Earth. Snorkeling or diving in Lake Tanganyika reveals a mesmerizing underwater world, teeming with colorful cichlids, catfish, and other aquatic creatures.

To the east lies the captivating Zanzibar Archipelago, a group of islands renowned for their pristine white-sand beaches, turquoise waters, and vibrant coral reefs. Zanzibar, the largest island, has a rich history shaped by a fusion of African, Arab, and European influences, offering visitors a cultural and historical experience unlike any other. The archipelago's charm extends beyond Zanzibar, with smaller islands like Pemba and Mafia boasting their own unique attractions, including tranquil coastal landscapes and exceptional diving opportunities.

Tanzania's geography is not limited to its mainland and islands. It is also home to the Great Rift Valley, a geological wonder that stretches across several countries in East Africa. The Tanzanian section of the Rift Valley encompasses stunning features such as the Ngorongoro Crater, a UNESCO World Heritage Site and a natural amphitheater teeming with an incredible concentration of wildlife. This ancient volcanic caldera is a testament to the raw power of nature, providing a haven for lions, elephants, zebras, and countless other species.

In conclusion, Tanzania's geographical marvels are nothing short of extraordinary. From the majestic heights of Mount Kilimanjaro to the crystal-clear waters of Lake Tanganyika and the idyllic beaches of Zanzibar, this country's diverse landscapes and natural wonders offer a captivating journey for those seeking adventure, beauty, and a deeper understanding of the world we inhabit.

Ancient Footsteps: Prehistoric Tanzania and the Origins of Humanity

In the vast landscapes of what is now Tanzania, deep in the annals of time, lies an extraordinary story that predates recorded history—the story of our shared human origins. Tanzania, with its rich archaeological heritage, holds a special place in unraveling the mysteries of our ancient past and shedding light on the evolution of our species.

The story begins millions of years ago, in the region known as the Olduvai Gorge. Located in northern Tanzania, this geological marvel has become synonymous with groundbreaking discoveries that have revolutionized our understanding of human evolution. The Olduvai Gorge has yielded a treasure trove of fossilized remains and ancient artifacts, painting a vivid picture of our ancestors' journey through time.

The Olduvai Gorge's significance was first realized by the pioneering work of husband-and-wife team Louis and Mary Leakey in the 1930s. Their meticulous excavations unearthed fossils of early hominins, revealing a lineage that predates modern humans. Among their remarkable finds were the remains of Australopithecus boisei, also known as "Nutcracker Man," and Homo habilis, the first known toolmakers.

The significance of these discoveries cannot be overstated. They provided crucial evidence of the existence of hominins in East Africa over two million years ago, highlighting Tanzania as a key location for understanding human evolution. The Olduvai Gorge continues to be an active site of exploration and continues to yield new insights into our ancestral past.

As we venture further into Tanzania's prehistoric history, we encounter another remarkable site—Laetoli. Located in the northeastern part of the country, Laetoli is famous for its extraordinary collection of hominin footprints. These footprints, preserved in volcanic ash, offer a tangible connection to our distant ancestors, showcasing their bipedal locomotion and providing valuable information about their behavior and social structures.

The Laetoli footprints, discovered by Mary Leakey in 1976, date back approximately 3.6 million years. They represent one of the earliest pieces of evidence of upright walking in hominins and provide crucial insights into the evolution of our species. The footprints suggest that our ancestors were already walking on two legs long before the development of more advanced tool-making abilities.

Moving forward in time, we encounter the enigmatic rock art of Kondoa. Located in central Tanzania, the Kondoa Rock Art Sites contain an astounding collection of ancient paintings and engravings, some dating back thousands of years. These artworks provide a window into the beliefs, rituals, and daily lives of the prehistoric peoples who once inhabited this region.

The Kondoa Rock Art Sites encompass over 150 different rock shelters, each adorned with intricate designs depicting a variety of subjects, including human figures, animals, and geometric patterns. These artistic expressions not only showcase the creativity and cultural richness of Tanzania's ancient inhabitants but also offer glimpses into their spiritual beliefs and social structures.

Further exploration of Tanzania's prehistoric past takes us to the Engaruka Basin, located in the Great Rift Valley. The Engaruka archaeological site presents the remnants of a sophisticated irrigation system built by an ancient civilization believed to have thrived between the 14th and 17th centuries. The ruins of terraced fields, stone enclosures, and canals bear witness to a highly organized society that flourished in an otherwise arid landscape.

The ingenuity of the Engaruka people is evident in their ability to harness water resources and cultivate crops in an otherwise challenging environment. Their advanced agricultural practices allowed them to sustain a thriving community, and their sophisticated social organization suggests a complex and hierarchical society.

As we delve into the ancient footsteps of prehistoric Tanzania, it becomes evident that this land has been a crucible of human existence since time immemorial. The archaeological wonders found within its borders paint a vivid picture of our shared ancestry and shed light on the remarkable journey that has led us to the present day.

Tanzania's rich prehistoric heritage, from the fossilized remains in the Olduvai Gorge to the Laetoli footprints, the Kondoa Rock Art Sites, and the ruins of Engaruka, all contribute to our collective understanding of human evolution and the diverse cultures that once thrived in this region. They remind us of our connection to the past and the importance of preserving and studying these ancient legacies for generations to come.

Zanzibar Archipelago: The Cradle of East African Civilization

Nestled off the coast of Tanzania lies the enchanting Zanzibar Archipelago, a group of islands that have played a pivotal role in shaping the history, culture, and trade of East Africa. With its pristine beaches, turquoise waters, and vibrant cultural heritage, the archipelago has earned its reputation as the "Cradle of East African Civilization."

The Zanzibar Archipelago consists of several islands, with the main ones being Unguja, commonly referred to as Zanzibar Island, and Pemba Island. These islands, along with smaller ones like Mafia Island, are known for their breathtaking beauty, warm tropical climate, and rich historical significance.

The archipelago's history dates back centuries, with evidence of human habitation dating as far back as the 1st century AD. Over the years, the islands of Zanzibar became a melting pot of cultures, attracting traders, explorers, and settlers from across the globe. Arab traders, Persian merchants, Indian Ocean seafarers, and European colonial powers all left their indelible marks on the archipelago's history and cultural heritage. One of the defining features of Zanzibar's history is its pivotal role in the Swahili civilization. The Swahili people, who are a Bantu-speaking ethnic group, have inhabited the East African coast for centuries, and Zanzibar became one of the most important centers of Swahili culture and trade. The archipelago served as a strategic hub for maritime trade routes, connecting Africa with the Arabian Peninsula, India, and beyond.

Zanzibar's strategic location made it a sought-after destination for traders, and it thrived as a trading post for goods such as spices, ivory, gold, and slaves. The archipelago's abundance of cloves, in particular, played a significant role in its history and economy, attracting merchants from as far as Persia and the Arab world. The Spice Islands, as they came to be known, brought immense wealth and prosperity to Zanzibar and the surrounding region.

The Arab influence is deeply ingrained in Zanzibar's cultural fabric. Stone Town, the historic heart of Zanzibar City and a UNESCO World Heritage Site, showcases the architectural legacy of the Arab traders and settlers. Its narrow, winding streets, intricately carved wooden doors, and ornate buildings with Arabesque designs create an atmospheric and evocative setting that transports visitors back in time.

Zanzibar's history took another significant turn in the 19th century with the arrival of European colonial powers. In 1840, Zanzibar became a protectorate of the Sultanate of Oman, solidifying its status as an important trading center. Later, in the late 19th century, Zanzibar fell under British colonial rule and became a key part of the British Empire's presence in East Africa.

The abolition of the slave trade in the late 19th century marked a turning point in Zanzibar's history. It was during this period that the archipelago's economy shifted towards other industries, such as cloves, coconuts, and tourism. The legacy of the slave trade is remembered and acknowledged through sites like the Anglican Cathedral Church of Christ, built on the former site of a slave market.

Today, the Zanzibar Archipelago is renowned for its natural beauty, cultural diversity, and warm hospitality. Its idyllic beaches, fringed by swaying palm trees, attract visitors from around the world who come to bask in the sun, swim in the crystal-clear waters, and indulge in water sports such as snorkeling and scuba diving.

Beyond the beaches, Zanzibar offers a wealth of cultural experiences. Visitors can explore spice plantations, immersing themselves in the aromatic world of cloves, nutmeg, cinnamon, and other exotic spices. They can also delve into the vibrant markets, where the air is filled with the bustling energy of traders selling colorful textiles, intricate handcrafted goods, and delectable street food.

The Zanzibar Archipelago is also home to a vibrant blend of cultures and traditions. Swahili is the predominant language spoken on the islands, reflecting the rich linguistic heritage of the region. The people of Zanzibar embrace their multicultural roots, and the island's festivals, such as the Zanzibar International Film Festival and the Mwaka Kogwa Festival, showcase the diverse artistic, musical, and culinary traditions that thrive in this unique corner of the world.

In conclusion, the Zanzibar Archipelago stands as a testament to the rich tapestry of East African civilization. From its ancient Swahili roots to its pivotal role in the spice trade and the enduring influence of Arab and European settlers, Zanzibar's history is a fascinating blend of cultures, traditions, and legacies. Today, as visitors walk its shores and immerse themselves in its vibrant atmosphere, they can't help but feel the echoes of the past and the enduring allure of this enchanting Cradle of East African Civilization.

The Swahili Coast: Traders, Explorers, and the Indian Ocean Influence

Stretching along the eastern shores of Africa lies the vibrant and culturally rich Swahili Coast. This coastal region, encompassing parts of modern-day Kenya, Tanzania, Mozambique, and Somalia, has been a melting pot of trade, exploration, and cultural exchange for centuries. Shaped by its unique blend of African, Arab, Persian, and Indian influences, the Swahili Coast has played a pivotal role in the history of East Africa and the wider Indian Ocean region.

The story of the Swahili Coast begins as early as the 1st century CE when it became a hub for maritime trade between Africa, the Middle East, and the Far East. The coastal cities of Kilwa, Mombasa, Lamu, Zanzibar, and Mogadishu became thriving centers of commerce, attracting traders from distant lands who sought to capitalize on the region's abundant resources and strategic location. Arab traders, particularly those from the Arabian Peninsula and the Persian Gulf, were among the first to establish strong ties with the Swahili Coast. They brought with them a rich cultural heritage, Islamic traditions, and a passion for maritime exploration. These traders settled along the coast, intermarrying with local African communities and laying the foundation for the emergence of a unique Swahili culture.

The Swahili people, descendants of these early intermingling communities, became skilled seafarers, traders, and architects of a thriving civilization. They developed a distinct language, Swahili, which served as a lingua franca for communication and trade along the coast. Swahili, influenced by Bantu languages and Arabic, became a testament to the multicultural nature of the region and continues to be spoken by millions today. Trade along the Swahili Coast flourished, driven by the exchange of goods such as ivory, gold, spices, timber, and exotic animal products. The coast became known for its vibrant marketplaces, where traders from diverse backgrounds bartered and conducted business. Coastal cities became renowned for their skilled artisans who produced intricate woodcarvings, pottery, textiles, and jewelry, reflecting the fusion of cultural influences.

One of the most prominent trading cities on the Swahili Coast was Kilwa, situated in what is now southern Tanzania. Kilwa's strategic location allowed it to control trade routes between the African interior and the Indian Ocean, making it a vital center of commerce and cultural exchange. The city grew wealthy and powerful, leaving behind impressive ruins that testify to its former glory, including the Great Mosque and the Palace of Husuni Kubwa. Another significant coastal city was Mombasa, located in present-day Kenya. Mombasa's prominence as a trading port attracted merchants from Arabia, Persia, India, and even as far as China. The city's Old Town, a UNESCO World Heritage Site, showcases the architectural remnants of its past, with intricately carved doors, narrow streets, and vibrant markets that evoke a sense of the city's rich history.

Zanzibar, an island off the coast of Tanzania, emerged as a pivotal trading post and a center of Swahili culture. It became a hub for the spice trade, particularly cloves, which brought great wealth and prosperity to the island. Zanzibar's Stone Town, with its labyrinthine streets and

Arabian-inspired architecture, stands as a living testament to the region's history and cultural heritage. The Swahili Coast was not only a hub for trade but also a gateway for explorers venturing into the unknown. Arab navigators, such as Ibn Battuta and Ahmad ibn Majid, sailed the Indian Ocean, charting new territories and establishing maritime routes. Their voyages opened up the East African coast to further exploration and trade, linking it to the broader Indian Ocean world.

The Swahili Coast's influence extended beyond commerce and exploration. Islamic traditions, introduced by Arab traders, took root and spread throughout the region, leaving a lasting impact on the coastal communities. Mosques and Islamic schools became centers of learning and spiritual guidance, fostering a deep sense of religious identity that endures to this day.

As the centuries passed, the Swahili Coast faced various challenges and shifts in power. European colonial powers, such as the Portuguese, the Omani Arabs, and later the British, established control over parts of the coast, leaving their own imprint on the region's history. However, the Swahili Coast's vibrant cultural heritage remained resilient, and the spirit of trade, exploration, and cultural fusion continues to thrive along its shores.

In conclusion, the Swahili Coast stands as a testament to the rich history of trade, exploration, and cultural exchange in East Africa. From its early connections with Arab traders to its role as a vibrant center of commerce, the Swahili Coast has been shaped by the influences of Africa, the Middle East, and the Far East. Today, it remains a captivating region that embodies the legacy of a diverse and interconnected world.

Great Empires: From the Shamba Kingdom to the Maravi Federation

In the annals of East African history, the rise and fall of great empires have left an indelible mark on the region's cultural and political landscape. From the Shamba Kingdom to the Maravi Federation, these empires have shaped the course of history, leaving a legacy that continues to resonate to this day.

The story begins with the Shamba Kingdom, also known as the Kingdom of Zimbabwe, which emerged around the 9th century in what is now present-day Zimbabwe, Mozambique, and parts of Malawi. The Shamba Kingdom was a formidable empire that controlled a vast territory, encompassing fertile lands and thriving trade routes. It is renowned for its impressive stone structures, such as the Great Zimbabwe ruins, which stand as a testament to the kingdom's architectural prowess and political power.

The Great Zimbabwe ruins, a UNESCO World Heritage Site, provide a glimpse into the wealth and sophistication of the Shamba Kingdom. The stone structures, built without mortar, showcase the kingdom's advanced engineering and construction techniques. These structures served as royal residences, administrative centers, and symbols of the kingdom's authority. Trade played a crucial role in the success of the Shamba Kingdom. The empire's strategic location along trade routes linking the interior of Africa to the coast allowed it to flourish as a hub of commerce. Gold, ivory, and copper were among the valuable commodities that flowed through its territories, attracting merchants from far and wide.

As the Shamba Kingdom declined in the 15th century, new empires and kingdoms emerged, vying for power and control over the region. One of these was the Mutapa Empire, which rose to prominence in the 15th century in what is now modern-day Zimbabwe and Mozambique. The Mutapa Empire, also known as the Monomotapa Empire, inherited and built upon the legacy of the Shamba Kingdom.

The Mutapa Empire, like its predecessor, relied on trade as a source of wealth and influence. It controlled the lucrative gold trade, establishing a network of trade routes that extended as far as the Swahili Coast and the Indian Ocean. The empire's rulers, known as Munhumutapa, held great power and were highly regarded by neighboring states and foreign traders. The Mutapa Empire thrived for several centuries, witnessing periods of expansion and decline. It reached its zenith in the 16th century under the reign of Matope Nyakunyati, who extended the empire's influence and established a centralized administration. The empire's decline came in the 17th century, as internal strife, external pressures, and the arrival of European colonizers weakened its authority.

While the Mutapa Empire waned, another empire rose to prominence in the region—the Maravi Empire. The Maravi Empire, sometimes referred to as the Maravi Federation, emerged in the 15th century and encompassed parts of present-day Malawi, Mozambique, and Tanzania. It was a confederation of various ethnic groups, including the Chewa, Nyanja, and Yao. The Maravi Empire was known for its military might and political organization. Its rulers, known as kalongas, commanded a formidable army and exercised control over a vast territory. The empire's capital,

Zomba, became a center of administration, trade, and cultural exchange.

Trade once again played a crucial role in the success of the Maravi Empire. The region's fertile lands, abundant natural resources, and proximity to the Indian Ocean facilitated trade with Arab and Swahili traders, who brought goods such as ivory, gold, and textiles. The empire's control over trade routes allowed it to accumulate wealth and exert influence over neighboring states.

The Maravi Empire's influence extended beyond politics and trade. It left a lasting impact on the region's cultural and linguistic heritage. The Chewa people, one of the prominent ethnic groups within the empire, continue to maintain their distinct cultural traditions and language to this day.

As European colonial powers encroached upon the region in the 19th century, the Maravi Empire, like other African empires, faced significant challenges. The empire eventually disintegrated under colonial rule, leading to the emergence of modern nation-states in the region.

In conclusion, the rise and fall of great empires from the Shamba Kingdom to the Maravi Federation highlight the dynamic and complex history of East Africa. These empires, through their political, economic, and cultural achievements, left an enduring legacy that continues to shape the region. They remind us of the rich tapestry of African history and the diverse civilizations that thrived on the continent long before the arrival of colonial powers.

Iron and Ivory: Trade and Expansion in Medieval Tanzania

In the medieval period, Tanzania's coastal regions witnessed a flourishing trade network that propelled economic growth, cultural exchange, and territorial expansion. This era, characterized by the trade in iron and ivory, left an indelible mark on Tanzania's history, shaping its social, economic, and political landscape.

Iron played a vital role in the medieval Tanzanian societies. Skilled blacksmiths forged iron tools, weapons, and implements that revolutionized agriculture, trade, and craftsmanship. The abundance of iron ore deposits in the region allowed for the production of high-quality iron, which became a valuable commodity sought after by both local communities and distant traders.

The production of iron tools and weapons enabled Tanzanian societies to cultivate the land more efficiently, leading to increased agricultural productivity. The adoption of iron hoes, axes, and plows transformed farming practices, facilitating the clearing of land, the cultivation of crops, and the expansion of agricultural settlements. The surplus food generated from these advances fueled population growth and contributed to the development of vibrant trading centers.

The trade in iron was closely linked to the expansion of territorial influence and the rise of powerful chiefdoms and city-states along the Tanzanian coast. These political entities, such as Kilwa, Sofala, and Mombasa, leveraged their control over iron production and trade to amass wealth, consolidate power, and assert dominance over neighboring regions. They became thriving centers of commerce, attracting merchants from distant lands who sought to obtain iron and other valuable goods.

Ivory, another highly prized commodity, played a significant role in the medieval trade networks of Tanzania. The region's abundant elephant populations provided a lucrative source of ivory, which was in high demand in international markets. Tanzanian ivory became a sought-after commodity, sought by Arab, Persian, Indian, and European traders.

The ivory trade stimulated economic growth, fostered cultural exchange, and contributed to the rise of powerful city-states. Coastal cities such as Kilwa, famous for its intricate carvings and ornate doors, emerged as key centers for ivory trade. These cities served as intermediaries between inland African communities, who hunted and supplied the ivory, and the international traders who transported it to markets across the globe.

The ivory trade not only brought economic prosperity but also led to cultural exchange and the diffusion of artistic and architectural styles. The demand for ivory carvings and artifacts fueled the growth of skilled artisans who produced intricate works of art, including jewelry, sculptures, and decorative objects. These artistic creations reflected the fusion of local African traditions with influences from the Arab world, Persia, and beyond.

The rise of powerful city-states along the Tanzanian coast was not without challenges. Competition for control over the lucrative iron and ivory trade routes often led to conflicts and power struggles. Rivalries between city-states, as well as incursions by external forces, such as the Portuguese in the 15th century, posed significant threats to the stability and autonomy of these coastal societies.

Despite these challenges, Tanzania's medieval period was a time of remarkable economic prosperity, cultural vibrancy, and territorial expansion. The iron and ivory trade networks that crisscrossed the region fostered connections between diverse communities, facilitating the exchange of goods, ideas, and cultural practices. The wealth accumulated from these trades fueled the growth of urban centers, the development of specialized crafts, and the rise of powerful political entities.

In conclusion, the medieval period in Tanzania was defined by the trade in iron and ivory, which shaped the region's history and propelled economic and cultural growth. The production and exchange of iron tools revolutionized agriculture and craftsmanship, while the demand for ivory stimulated trade, artistic expression, and territorial expansion. The legacy of this era can still be seen today in the vibrant coastal cities, the intricate carvings, and the cultural diversity that flourishes along Tanzania's historic trade routes.

Kilwa Kisiwani: East Africa's Medieval Trading Powerhouse

In the waters of the Indian Ocean, off the coast of present-day Tanzania, lies the historic island of Kilwa Kisiwani. This small but mighty island became a renowned trading powerhouse during the medieval period, commanding vast wealth and influence along the East African coast. Kilwa Kisiwani's rise to prominence as a bustling center of commerce and culture left an indelible mark on the region's history.

Kilwa Kisiwani's strategic location made it an ideal hub for maritime trade. Situated on an island just off the Tanzanian mainland, it offered natural harbors and easy access to the open sea. This advantageous position allowed Kilwa Kisiwani to become a pivotal link in the vast network of Indian Ocean trade routes, connecting East Africa with the Arabian Peninsula, Persia, India, and beyond.

The prosperity of Kilwa Kisiwani was fueled by its control over valuable commodities, particularly gold, ivory, and spices. Gold, mined from the interior regions of East Africa, flowed through Kilwa Kisiwani, attracting merchants from distant lands who sought to acquire this precious metal. Ivory, harvested from the abundant elephant populations of the region, was another highly prized commodity that passed through the island's bustling markets. Additionally, Kilwa Kisiwani played a role in the spice trade, capitalizing on the region's abundant cloves, cinnamon, and other aromatic treasures.

Under the Kilwa Sultanate, which emerged in the 10th century, Kilwa Kisiwani experienced a period of unprecedented growth and prosperity. The sultans of Kilwa, known as the Mwenemutapas, governed the island and its vast territories, wielding immense political power and establishing a centralized administration. The sultans leveraged their control over trade and resources to amass wealth and build a magnificent city that became a beacon of opulence and architectural grandeur.

One of the most impressive architectural legacies of Kilwa Kisiwani is the Great Mosque. Constructed in the 12th century, it stands as a testament to the city's prominence and Islamic cultural influence. The Great Mosque, with its intricate coral stone walls and imposing minaret, served as a center of worship and a symbol of the city's religious and political authority.

The prosperity of Kilwa Kisiwani is also evident in the ruins of grand palaces and residences that dot the island. These structures, adorned with decorative carvings and ornate details, bear witness to the luxurious lifestyles enjoyed by the ruling elite of the Kilwa Sultanate. The Palace of Husuni Kubwa, with its vast courtyard and multiple stories, stands as a remarkable example of the architectural prowess and grandeur of the era.

The success of Kilwa Kisiwani was not limited to its economic and political might. The city also became a hub of cultural exchange, attracting scholars, artists, and intellectuals from across the Indian Ocean world. Kilwa Kisiwani's cosmopolitan atmosphere fostered a vibrant intellectual and artistic scene, with a fusion of African, Arab, Persian, and Indian influences. This cross-cultural pollination enriched the city's traditions, artistic expressions, and social fabric.

The decline of Kilwa Kisiwani came in the 16th century, as external pressures and shifts in trade routes began to take their toll. The arrival of the Portuguese in the region disrupted the existing trade dynamics, leading to the decline of Kilwa's influence. The city's decline was further exacerbated by political instability and the emergence of competing powers along the East African coast.

Today, the ruins of Kilwa Kisiwani stand as a UNESCO World Heritage Site, a testament to the city's former glory. They serve as a reminder of the remarkable achievements of the Kilwa Sultanate and the city's pivotal role in the medieval trade networks of East Africa. The ruins, with their evocative atmosphere and historical significance, continue to captivate visitors, allowing them to glimpse into the rich tapestry of Kilwa Kisiwani's past.

In conclusion, Kilwa Kisiwani emerged as a medieval trading powerhouse, commanding wealth, and influence along the East African coast. Its strategic location, control over valuable commodities, and architectural grandeur propelled it to become a center of commerce, culture, and political power. Kilwa Kisiwani's legacy as a vibrant cosmopolitan city and a testament to East Africa's rich medieval history continues to fascinate and inspire generations.

The Arab Influence: Omani Sultans and the Rise of Zanzibar

The influence of Arab traders and settlers in East Africa reached its zenith with the rise of the Omani Sultans and the establishment of Zanzibar as a major center of power and trade. The Arab influence, particularly from the Sultanate of Oman, played a significant role in shaping the history, culture, and economy of Zanzibar.

The roots of the Omani Sultanate's involvement in East Africa can be traced back to the 17th century when Omani Arabs began to establish a presence along the Swahili Coast. They saw the strategic potential of the region, with its valuable trade routes, abundance of resources, and access to the Indian Ocean. Seeking to expand their influence, the Omani Sultans set their sights on Zanzibar, an island that held immense promise.

In the late 17th century, the Omani Sultanate seized control of Zanzibar and made it their stronghold in East Africa. Zanzibar's strategic location, natural harbors, and fertile lands made it an ideal base for trade, exploration, and expansion. Under Omani rule, Zanzibar thrived as a center of commerce, attracting merchants from Arabia, Persia, India, and beyond.

The Omani Sultans recognized the economic potential of Zanzibar's resources, particularly cloves. The island's climate and soil conditions proved ideal for cultivating this highly sought-after spice. The Omani Sultans established extensive clove plantations, transforming Zanzibar into the

"Spice Island" and catapulting it into a position of global importance in the spice trade.

Zanzibar's prominence in the spice trade brought immense wealth to the Omani Sultans and propelled the island's growth and development. The Sultans, known as the Sayyids, ruled over Zanzibar from their palace in Stone Town, overseeing a vast empire that extended from the Swahili Coast to parts of modern-day Kenya, Mozambique, and Madagascar. They fostered an environment conducive to trade, encouraging merchants from different parts of the world to converge on the island.

Under Omani rule, Zanzibar became a melting pot of cultures and traditions. The Arab influence permeated all aspects of life on the island, from language and religion to architecture and cuisine. The Omani rulers brought with them Islamic traditions and Arab customs, which merged with the existing Swahili culture to create a unique and vibrant blend.

Stone Town, the historic heart of Zanzibar, showcases the architectural legacy of the Arab influence. Its narrow, winding streets are lined with intricately carved wooden doors, elegant townhouses, and mosques adorned with ornate domes and minarets. The fusion of Arab and Swahili architectural styles in Stone Town creates an atmospheric and evocative setting, reflecting the cultural interplay that defines Zanzibar.

The Arab influence extended beyond trade and architecture. Zanzibar's embrace of Islam deepened under Omani rule, with the construction of numerous mosques and Islamic schools. The religion became a unifying force, shaping the island's social fabric and fostering a sense of community among its diverse inhabitants.

The Omani Sultans' reign in Zanzibar came to an end in the late 19th century with the arrival of European colonial powers. The British established a protectorate over Zanzibar, leading to a shift in power dynamics and the erosion of Omani influence. However, the Arab legacy and the impact of Omani rule remained deeply ingrained in the identity and culture of Zanzibar.

Today, Zanzibar stands as a testament to the Arab influence and the Omani Sultans' legacy. Its vibrant culture, architectural wonders, and spice trade heritage continue to captivate visitors from around the world. The Arab influence, interwoven with the Swahili and African traditions, has shaped Zanzibar into a unique destination that preserves the rich history of East Africa's connection with the Arab world.

In conclusion, the Omani Sultans and the Arab influence played a pivotal role in the rise of Zanzibar as a center of power and trade in East Africa. Their vision and leadership transformed Zanzibar into a thriving hub of commerce, culture, and diversity. The legacy of their rule can still be seen and felt in the vibrant atmosphere of Zanzibar today, perpetuating the island's rich history and cultural heritage.

European Intrusions: Portuguese Explorers and Coastal Dominance

The arrival of Portuguese explorers on the shores of East Africa marked a significant turning point in the region's history. These intrepid seafarers, driven by the quest for riches and a desire to establish trade routes to the East, made their presence felt along the coastal regions, challenging existing powers and reshaping the dynamics of the Indian Ocean trade.

The Portuguese, led by Vasco da Gama, first reached East Africa in 1498 when they landed in what is now modern-day Mozambique. Their arrival heralded a new era of European exploration and influence in the region. The Portuguese were eager to establish a monopoly over the spice trade, which had been dominated by Arab and Indian merchants for centuries.

The Portuguese navigators' ambitions extended beyond trade. They sought to establish political control over key coastal cities and gain a foothold in the lucrative Indian Ocean trade network. This desire for dominance led to conflicts with existing powers, including the city-states of the Swahili Coast and the Arab traders who held significant influence in the region.

In their pursuit of dominance, the Portuguese employed a combination of military force, alliances, and strategic fortifications. They established a string of fortified trading posts along the East African coast, including Sofala, Kilwa, and Mombasa. These forts, designed to protect Portuguese interests and control trade routes, became symbols of European presence and influence.

The Portuguese not only sought control over trade but also aimed to spread Christianity throughout the region. They sent missionaries to convert the local populations, resulting in the establishment of Catholic missions in various coastal towns. However, the conversion efforts faced resistance from the predominantly Muslim inhabitants, leading to tensions and conflicts.

The Portuguese dominance in the region was not without challenges. Rival European powers, most notably the Dutch and the British, sought to undermine Portuguese control and establish their own footholds in the Indian Ocean trade. The Dutch, in particular, launched a series of attacks on Portuguese strongholds, eventually driving them out of many strategic locations.

Despite these challenges, the Portuguese legacy in East Africa remains significant. Their arrival marked the beginning of a new chapter in the region's history, characterized by European intrusion and the gradual erosion of indigenous powers. Portuguese influence left an indelible mark on the coastal architecture, language, and cultural practices of the region.

The influence of the Portuguese can be seen in the architectural remnants of their forts and trading posts, such as Fort Jesus in Mombasa. These structures, built with European design principles and materials, stand as enduring symbols of the European presence in East Africa. They serve as reminders of the struggles for dominance and the clash of cultures that defined this period.

The Portuguese also left their mark on the Swahili language. Loanwords from Portuguese entered the Swahili lexicon, reflecting the linguistic exchange that took place between the two cultures. The introduction of new vocabulary related to trade, maritime activities, and European concepts enriched the Swahili language and provided a lasting testament to this period of European intrusion.

The arrival of the Portuguese and subsequent European powers had far-reaching consequences for East Africa. The region experienced significant political, economic, and social transformations as indigenous powers adapted to the changing dynamics and power structures. The intrusion of Europeans into the Indian Ocean trade network laid the groundwork for future colonial domination and shaped the trajectory of East African history.

In conclusion, the Portuguese explorers' arrival and their subsequent dominance along the East African coast marked a critical juncture in the region's history. Their quest for trade, political control, and religious influence reshaped the dynamics of the Indian Ocean trade and set the stage for further European intrusions. The Portuguese legacy, while complex and often contentious, continues to shape the cultural and historical narrative of East Africa.

The Majestic Maasai: Warriors and Nomadic Pastoralists

In the vast landscapes of East Africa, the Maasai people have carved out a distinct and enduring cultural identity. Renowned for their warrior traditions, vibrant clothing, and nomadic pastoral lifestyle, the Maasai have captivated the imagination of people around the world. This chapter delves into the rich history and unique characteristics of the Maasai, shedding light on their customs, beliefs, and their profound connection to the land.

The Maasai are an indigenous ethnic group primarily inhabiting parts of Kenya and Tanzania, with smaller populations in Uganda and Ethiopia. They are part of the larger Nilotic ethnic group, which includes various other communities across East Africa. The Maasai people have a long and storied history, with roots dating back centuries.

Historically, the Maasai were semi-nomadic pastoralists, relying on livestock, particularly cattle, as the cornerstone of their livelihood. Their ability to thrive in the often harsh and arid landscapes of East Africa is a testament to their deep understanding of the land and their close relationship with their livestock. Cattle, in Maasai culture, represent not only wealth and status but also spiritual and cultural significance.

The Maasai's nomadic lifestyle, coupled with their strong warrior traditions, allowed them to navigate and protect their herds in the face of environmental challenges and conflicts with neighboring communities. The Maasai warriors, known as morans, were revered for their bravery, physical prowess, and deep sense of honor. The morans underwent rigorous training, honing their skills in combat, spear throwing, and other traditional weaponry.

Traditional Maasai attire is a vibrant reflection of their cultural heritage. Both men and women adorn themselves with distinctive clothing and jewelry. The Maasai are known for their bright red, blue, and purple shuka, a traditional cloth worn as a robe or wrapped around the body. Intricate beadwork, crafted by Maasai women, adorns their necks, arms, and ears, symbolizing beauty, identity, and cultural pride.

Maasai society is organized into age-sets, with individuals progressing through various stages of life and responsibilities. Elders hold a revered status within the community, as they are considered the custodians of Maasai customs, oral traditions, and ancestral wisdom. Decision-making is often guided by a council of elders, ensuring the preservation of Maasai cultural values and the collective well-being of the community.

Spirituality is deeply ingrained in Maasai life. The Maasai believe in a higher power known as Enkai or Ngai, who is believed to control the natural world and all living things. The Maasai maintain a strong spiritual connection to the land, considering it sacred and central to their existence. Rituals, ceremonies, and prayers are conducted to seek blessings, ensure fertility, and express gratitude to Enkai.

While the Maasai have maintained their cultural practices and way of life for generations, they have also faced challenges in the face of modernization, land disputes, and social changes. Increased pressure on land resources, encroachment from agricultural expansion, and the impact of globalization have posed significant challenges to the Maasai's traditional pastoral lifestyle.

However, the Maasai people have shown remarkable resilience and adaptability. They have been actively engaged in advocating for their rights, land preservation, and the protection of their cultural heritage. Many Maasai communities have embraced education and economic opportunities while striving to maintain their traditional values and practices.

The Maasai's unique cultural identity and their iconic presence in East Africa make them an integral part of the region's cultural tapestry. Their vibrant traditions, close connection to the land, and indomitable spirit continue to inspire admiration and fascination. The Maasai people stand as a testament to the richness and diversity of Africa's cultural heritage and the importance of preserving indigenous traditions in an ever-changing world.

In conclusion, the Maasai people embody the majesty and resilience of East Africa's warrior pastoralists. Their nomadic lifestyle, warrior traditions, and vibrant cultural expressions have captivated the world's attention. Through their deep spiritual connection to the land, the Maasai have carved out a place in history as custodians of their ancestral heritage and as a symbol of Africa's rich cultural tapestry.

Slave Trade and Abolition: Tanzania's Role in the Global Struggle

The transatlantic slave trade, one of the darkest chapters in human history, had a profound impact on Tanzania and the wider East African region. For centuries, East Africa served as a source, transit, and export hub for enslaved people, with Tanzania playing a significant role in this tragic trade. However, Tanzania also became a battleground in the global struggle for the abolition of slavery, with individuals and communities making significant contributions to the eventual eradication of this heinous institution.

The origins of the slave trade in East Africa can be traced back to pre-colonial times when Arab traders established commercial networks along the Swahili Coast. These traders, primarily from Oman and other Arabian regions, sought slaves as a valuable commodity to meet the demands of the Middle Eastern and Indian Ocean markets. Slavery was deeply embedded in the social, economic, and political fabric of the region.

Tanzania, with its vast coastline and proximity to the Indian Ocean trade routes, became a key link in the transcontinental slave trade. Arab traders, through extensive networks and alliances with local African intermediaries, acquired enslaved people from the interior regions and transported them to coastal ports. From there, enslaved individuals were shipped across the Indian Ocean to destinations as far-reaching as the Arabian Peninsula, Persia, and India.

The impact of the slave trade on Tanzania cannot be overstated. Entire communities were uprooted and torn apart, families were separated, and human lives were commodified and dehumanized. The scale of the trade varied over time, with periods of intensified enslavement coinciding with increased demands from external markets. Coastal communities, such as Bagamoyo, Kilwa, and Zanzibar, were particularly affected, serving as major slave markets and transit points.

However, amidst this grim reality, Tanzania also became a site of resistance and defiance against the institution of slavery. The struggle for abolition gained momentum in the 19th century, as the voices of activists and abolitionists grew louder across the globe. Tanzania became a significant battleground in this fight, with both local and international forces working towards ending the slave trade.

One of the most notable figures in Tanzania's fight against slavery was the Arab trader turned abolitionist, Tippu Tip. Born in Zanzibar, Tippu Tip initially profited from the slave trade but later renounced his involvement and became a prominent advocate for the abolitionist cause. He played a crucial role in challenging the entrenched systems of enslavement and working towards the eradication of the trade in East Africa.

Tanzanian communities also played an important part in the resistance against slavery. Uprising and rebellions by enslaved individuals, such as the Mazrui uprising in the late 19th century, demonstrated the determination of the oppressed to secure their freedom. These acts of resistance, coupled with the international pressure to end the transatlantic slave trade, contributed to the eventual abolition of slavery in Tanzania and the wider East African region.

The formal abolition of slavery in Tanzania came in the late 19th century, as European colonial powers exerted greater control over the region. The German and British colonial administrations, while pursuing their own political and economic interests, enacted legislation and implemented policies aimed at curbing the slave trade. This marked a significant turning point in Tanzania's history, as the chains of slavery were gradually broken.

The legacy of slavery and its abolition continues to shape Tanzania's social fabric. Descendants of enslaved individuals, who make up a significant portion of the population, have worked tirelessly to preserve their cultural heritage and reclaim their identity. Efforts have been made to document and commemorate the history of slavery, such as the establishment of museums and cultural centers, ensuring that this painful past is not forgotten.

In conclusion, Tanzania's role in the transatlantic slave trade cannot be overlooked. The region was deeply impacted by the trade in enslaved people, with devastating consequences for communities and individuals. However, Tanzania also became a battleground in the global struggle for abolition, with local activists and international forces working towards the eradication of slavery. The legacy of this period continues to shape Tanzania's present, as efforts to preserve history and promote social justice pave the way for a more inclusive and equitable future.

German East Africa: Colonial Ambitions and Resistance

The late 19th century witnessed a scramble for Africa as European powers sought to expand their colonial empires. Germany, eager to secure its share of the African continent, set its sights on East Africa, establishing German East Africa (Deutsch-Ostafrika) as a colony. This chapter explores the colonial ambitions of Germany, the impact of their rule on the region, and the resistance that arose in response to German colonialism.

Germany's interest in East Africa was driven by economic, political, and strategic motives. The colony of German East Africa, which encompassed present-day Tanzania, Rwanda, and Burundi, offered vast resources, including valuable minerals, fertile lands, and access to the Indian Ocean trade routes. The German government saw the potential for economic exploitation and sought to establish control over the region.

In 1884, the German explorer Carl Peters signed a series of controversial treaties with local chiefs, claiming vast territories on behalf of the German Empire. These treaties, often obtained through coercion and dubious means, laid the foundation for German colonial rule in East Africa. The German administration, headed by the German East Africa Company, embarked on a mission to exploit the region's resources and establish control over the local population.

German rule in East Africa was marked by a systematic exploitation of resources and the imposition of colonial administration. Plantations were established, primarily for the cultivation of cash crops such as cotton and sisal, leading to the forced labor of local Africans. The German administration also aimed to promote settler colonialism, encouraging German nationals to migrate to East Africa and establish agricultural ventures.

The impact of German colonialism on the local population was severe. Africans were subjected to forced labor, heavy taxation, and harsh treatment. Land rights were disregarded, and traditional African institutions were undermined. This exploitation and oppression sparked widespread resistance among the indigenous population.

One of the most notable figures in the resistance against German colonialism was Chief Mkwawa of the Hehe people. Chief Mkwawa fiercely opposed German rule, leading his people in a protracted guerrilla war against the German forces. Despite facing overwhelming odds, Mkwawa's resistance demonstrated the determination and resilience of the local population against colonial oppression.

Resistance to German colonial rule was not limited to armed conflict. Africans employed various forms of protest and subversion, including labor strikes, boycotts, and the preservation of cultural practices. These acts of resistance aimed to challenge the German administration's authority and assert the dignity and rights of the African population.

The German colonial project in East Africa faced significant challenges, both from within and outside the region. The harsh conditions, including disease, rugged terrain, and resistance from local communities, made governance and economic exploitation difficult. Moreover, Germany faced competition and conflicts with neighboring

European powers, such as the British and the Portuguese, who sought to protect their own colonial interests.

German colonial rule in East Africa came to an end during World War I when British and Belgian forces launched offensives to seize German territories. In 1916, German East Africa fell to the British, marking the end of German colonial ambitions in the region. The former German colony was then placed under British administration as the territory of Tanganyika.

The legacy of German colonialism in Tanzania is complex and multifaceted. The period of German rule left lasting scars on the local population, with deep socio-economic inequalities and cultural disruptions that continue to be felt today. However, the resistance to German colonialism also fostered a spirit of defiance, unity, and pride among Tanzanians, laying the groundwork for the eventual struggle for independence.

In conclusion, German colonial rule in East Africa, particularly in German East Africa, was characterized by economic exploitation, repression, and resistance. The German administration sought to extract resources, impose their authority, and promote settler colonialism. However, resistance from local communities, exemplified by figures like Chief Mkwawa, demonstrated the resilience and determination of the African population in the face of oppression. The legacy of German colonialism continues to shape Tanzania's history and serves as a reminder of the struggles endured and the resilience displayed by the people of East Africa.

Maji Maji Rebellion: Tanzanian Resistance against German Rule

One of the most significant chapters in Tanzania's history of resistance against colonialism is the Maji Maji Rebellion, a mass uprising that erupted in the early 20th century in response to German colonial rule. The rebellion, named after the Swahili term for "water," symbolized the people's belief in the spiritual power of protective waters against the German bullets. This chapter delves into the causes, events, and legacy of the Maji Maji Rebellion, highlighting its significance in Tanzania's struggle for independence.

The seeds of the rebellion were sown during the late 19th century as the German administration imposed heavy taxation, forced labor, and exploitative agricultural policies on the local population. These oppressive measures, coupled with the loss of land and the erosion of traditional authority, created a fertile ground for resistance to germinate. The spark that ignited the rebellion was the imposition of the cotton tax, which compelled Africans to cultivate cotton for the German authorities. This tax placed an enormous burden on the already impoverished population, who were forced to toil on cotton fields instead of tending to their own subsistence crops. The discontent among the people grew, and a movement of resistance began to take shape.

The rebellion gained momentum in 1905 when Kinjikitile Ngwale, a spiritual leader and medium, emerged as a charismatic figure rallying the people against German oppression. Ngwale, believed to possess supernatural powers, preached a message of unity and resistance, asserting that by performing spiritual rituals and using a magic potion known as "Maji Maji," the people would become invincible and impervious to German bullets. The Maji Maji Rebellion quickly spread across the southern regions of Tanzania, encompassing numerous ethnic groups and communities. The rebellion united people from different backgrounds under a shared purpose: to liberate themselves from the oppressive rule of the Germans and reclaim their land, freedom, and dignity.

The rebels, armed with traditional weapons such as spears, bows, and arrows, launched attacks against German military outposts, plantations, and administrative centers. They employed guerilla warfare tactics, utilizing their knowledge of the local terrain and taking advantage of the element of surprise. The rebels also targeted collaborators and local African chiefs who aligned themselves with the German administration.

The German response to the rebellion was brutal and marked by extreme violence. They deployed a combination of military might, aerial bombardment, and scorched-earth tactics to quell the uprising. Villages were destroyed, crops were burned, and the civilian population was subjected to reprisals and collective punishment.

The rebellion, although ultimately suppressed by the overwhelming military force of the Germans, inflicted significant casualties on both sides. Estimates vary, but it is believed that tens of thousands of Tanzanians lost their lives during the course of the rebellion, including combatants and civilians caught in the crossfire or subjected to German atrocities.

The legacy of the Maji Maji Rebellion is profound and far-reaching. Despite its ultimate military defeat, the rebellion left an indelible mark on Tanzanian history and became a symbol of resistance against colonial oppression. It inspired subsequent generations of Tanzanian nationalists and freedom fighters who continued the struggle for independence.

The Maji Maji Rebellion exposed the inherent weaknesses and injustices of the German colonial system. It revealed the resilience and bravery of the African people, who were willing to lay down their lives in the fight for freedom. The rebellion also underscored the importance of unity among diverse ethnic groups in Tanzania, setting a precedent for future nationalist movements.

The legacy of the Maji Maji Rebellion can be seen in Tanzania's journey towards independence. The memory of the rebellion served as a rallying cry for nationalists, shaping their determination to overthrow colonial rule and establish an independent Tanzania. The rebellion also highlighted the significance of cultural heritage and spirituality in the struggle for liberation, influencing the development of a national identity rooted in African traditions and values.

In conclusion, the Maji Maji Rebellion stands as a testament to the resilience, bravery, and determination of the Tanzanian people in their fight against German colonial rule. The rebellion, fueled by grievances over oppressive policies and a longing for freedom, left an indelible mark on Tanzania's history. It serves as a reminder of the sacrifices made by those who came before and the ongoing struggle for justice, freedom, and self-determination.

British Rule and Independence Movements: Striving for Autonomy

Following the defeat of German forces in World War I, Tanzania, then known as Tanganyika, came under British administration as a League of Nations mandate. British rule in Tanganyika, which lasted for several decades, witnessed the growth of nationalist movements and a gradual shift towards self-governance. This chapter explores the era of British rule in Tanzania and the emergence of independence movements, highlighting the aspirations and struggles of Tanzanians in their pursuit of autonomy.

British rule in Tanganyika commenced in 1916, following the ousting of German forces during World War I. The British administration initially focused on consolidating control and implementing reforms aimed at improving governance, infrastructure, and economic development. Tanganyika was administered as a British mandate under the authority of the League of Nations until the mandate system was replaced by the United Nations Trusteeship in 1946.

During the early years of British rule, the impact of colonial policies on the local population was mixed. While some positive changes were introduced, such as improved healthcare, education, and infrastructure, the overall framework of colonial control remained intact. Indigenous Tanzanians continued to face political, economic, and social marginalization under the British administration.

The advent of World War II brought significant changes to the colonial landscape, igniting a sense of political awakening among Tanzanians. The war exerted strains on the colonial powers and exposed the contradictions of European imperialism. Tanzanian soldiers, serving in the British military, were exposed to new ideas and experiences, which further fueled nationalist sentiments upon their return to Tanganyika.

The post-war period witnessed the emergence of nationalist movements in Tanganyika, with the Tanganyika African Association (TAA) at the forefront. The TAA, led by figures such as Julius Nyerere, Oscar Kambona, and Abdulrahman Mohamed Babu, advocated for greater political representation and the pursuit of independence. These early nationalist leaders played a crucial role in galvanizing the aspirations of Tanzanians and challenging colonial authority.

The British administration, initially resistant to demands for self-governance, gradually responded to the growing nationalist sentiment. A series of constitutional reforms were implemented, culminating in the establishment of a Legislative Council in 1945, which included elected African representatives. This marked a significant step towards political inclusion and provided a platform for Tanzanian voices to be heard.

As nationalist movements gained momentum, the struggle for independence intensified. The Tanganyika African National Union (TANU), formed in 1954 under the leadership of Julius Nyerere, emerged as a dominant force in the fight for self-rule. TANU aimed to unite Tanzanians across ethnic, regional, and religious lines, fostering a sense of national unity and collective action.

The road to independence was not without challenges. The British administration employed divide-and-rule tactics, seeking to exploit ethnic and regional divisions within Tanzanian society. However, the nationalist movement remained resilient, driven by a shared vision of a free and independent Tanzania.

In 1961, Tanganyika achieved independence from British colonial rule, with Julius Nyerere becoming the country's first Prime Minister. The transition to independence was relatively peaceful, and Tanganyika became a beacon of hope and inspiration for other African nations struggling for liberation.

The legacy of British rule in Tanzania is multifaceted. While the British administration left behind some enduring infrastructure, such as roads, railways, and educational institutions, the overall impact of colonialism on Tanzanian society was characterized by exploitation, inequality, and cultural disruption. The nationalist movements that emerged during this period laid the foundation for the vision of an independent and unified Tanzania.

The struggle for independence in Tanganyika also had a profound impact on the broader African continent. Tanzania became a staunch advocate for Pan-Africanism and played a pivotal role in supporting liberation movements in neighboring countries. Julius Nyerere, through his philosophy of Ujamaa, advocated for African socialism and self-reliance, inspiring a generation of leaders across Africa.

In conclusion, the era of British rule in Tanganyika witnessed the rise of nationalist movements and the quest for autonomy. Tanzanians, inspired by the spirit of independence sweeping across the African continent, fought against colonial oppression and worked towards the establishment of a free and self-governing nation. The struggles and aspirations of Tanzanians during this period laid the groundwork for the birth of an independent Tanzania and left an enduring legacy of resilience, unity, and the pursuit of self-determination.

The Birth of Tanganyika: Nyerere and the Struggle for Independence

Julius Kambarage Nyerere, a towering figure in Tanzania's history, played a pivotal role in leading the country to independence and shaping its early years as an independent nation. This chapter explores Nyerere's journey, his philosophy, and the struggle for independence that culminated in the birth of Tanganyika.

Born on April 13, 1922, in Butiama, Nyerere grew up in a rural village in present-day Tanzania. He received a quality education, attending local mission schools and later pursuing higher studies in Uganda and the United Kingdom. Nyerere's education exposed him to ideas of social justice, equality, and self-determination, which would shape his political ideology and vision for Tanganyika. Upon his return to Tanganyika in the early 1950s, Nyerere became actively involved in nationalist politics. In 1954, he played a key role in founding the Tanganyika African National Union (TANU), a political party that would spearhead the struggle for independence. Nyerere's leadership qualities, charisma, and dedication to the cause quickly made him the face of the independence movement.

Nyerere's political philosophy was grounded in the concept of African socialism, which he termed Ujamaa. He believed in the importance of communal values, collective responsibility, and equitable distribution of resources. Nyerere envisioned a society where Tanzanians would work together for the common good, embracing self-reliance and rejecting the pitfalls of capitalism and tribalism. Under Nyerere's leadership, TANU mobilized Tanzanians across ethnic, regional, and religious lines. The party's message of unity resonated deeply with the population, as it offered a vision of a harmonious and inclusive Tanganyika. TANU focused on grassroots organizing, empowering ordinary Tanzanians, and challenging the injustices perpetuated by colonialism.

The struggle for independence intensified throughout the late 1950s and early 1960s. Nyerere, along with other nationalist leaders, engaged in negotiations with the British administration to chart a path towards self-rule. Tanganyika's journey to independence was marked by a commitment to peaceful means, avoiding the violent upheavals that plagued some other African nations.

On December 9, 1961, Tanganyika achieved independence from British colonial rule. Julius Nyerere became the country's first Prime Minister, assuming the responsibility of guiding the newly independent nation. Tanganyika's independence marked a significant milestone in the African liberation movement and inspired hope for other nations still struggling for self-determination.

Nyerere's leadership during the early years of Tanganyika's independence was characterized by his unwavering commitment to democracy, social justice, and inclusive governance. He implemented policies aimed at national development, including education reforms, land redistribution, and the promotion of rural development. Nyerere also championed the rights of marginalized groups, such as women and minority communities, and sought to create a society where all Tanzanians could thrive.

One of Nyerere's most ambitious initiatives was the Arusha Declaration, unveiled in 1967. The declaration outlined a vision for socialist transformation in Tanzania, with an emphasis on rural development, collective farming, and the eradication of poverty. The Arusha Declaration encapsulated Nyerere's commitment to Ujamaa and served as a guiding framework for Tanzania's socio-economic development.

Nyerere's influence extended beyond the borders of Tanzania. He played a prominent role in Pan-Africanism and was a founding member of the Organization of African Unity (OAU), now known as the African Union. Nyerere advocated for African unity, economic cooperation, and the resolution of conflicts through peaceful means. His statesmanship and wisdom made him a respected leader on the global stage.

Julius Nyerere stepped down as President in 1985 after leading Tanzania for over two decades. Despite challenges and setbacks, his legacy as the founding father of the nation endures. Nyerere's vision of unity, self-reliance, and social justice continues to shape Tanzania's development trajectory. His emphasis on education, rural development, and participatory governance has left a lasting impact on Tanzanian society.

In conclusion, Julius Nyerere's leadership and the struggle for independence paved the way for the birth of Tanganyika as an independent nation. His political philosophy of Ujamaa, commitment to social justice, and dedication to African unity made him a revered figure in Tanzania and across the continent. Nyerere's legacy continues to resonate, as Tanzania strives to build upon his vision of an inclusive, prosperous, and united nation.

Zanzibar Revolution: Overthrowing the Sultanate

The Zanzibar Revolution of 1964 stands as a significant event in Tanzanian history, as it marked the overthrow of the Arab-dominated Sultanate and the establishment of a new government. This chapter explores the causes, events, and aftermath of the Zanzibar Revolution, shedding light on its impact and significance in shaping the socio-political landscape of Zanzibar and Tanzania as a whole.

Zanzibar, an archipelago off the coast of Tanzania, had a long history as a center of trade and influence in the Indian Ocean. The Arab Sultanate of Zanzibar, led by the ruling Arab elite, held power over the islands for centuries. However, by the mid-20th century, tensions and grievances had built up among the majority African population, which felt marginalized and excluded from political power.

The catalyst for the revolution was the electoral victory of the Afro-Shirazi Party (ASP) in July 1963. The ASP, representing the interests of the African majority, advocated for political and social reforms, including land redistribution, educational opportunities, and an end to racial discrimination. The election results signaled a desire for change among the population and heightened tensions with the ruling elite.

The revolution itself erupted on the night of January 12, 1964, when a group of revolutionaries launched a coordinated attack on key government buildings, including the Sultan's palace. The revolutionaries, consisting of members of the ASP, trade unions, and disaffected youth, sought to end the oppressive rule of the Sultanate and establish a new government that would address the needs and aspirations of the African population.

The revolution unfolded rapidly, with the sultan's forces quickly overwhelmed by the determined revolutionaries. The Sultan and his supporters, including Arab elites and loyalists, either fled or were captured. The revolutionaries declared victory and established the People's Republic of Zanzibar, led by Abeid Karume, a prominent figure in the Afro-Shirazi Party.

The aftermath of the revolution was marked by significant changes in Zanzibar's socio-political landscape. The new government embarked on a program of radical reforms, including the nationalization of land and industries, the implementation of social welfare programs, and the promotion of African cultural and political identity. The revolution also led to the expulsion of the Arab and South Asian communities, who were viewed as collaborators with the former Sultanate.

The Zanzibar Revolution had a ripple effect beyond the archipelago, shaping the political trajectory of Tanzania as a whole. In April 1964, Zanzibar merged with mainland Tanganyika to form the United Republic of Tanzania, with Julius Nyerere as its President. The revolution served as a catalyst for the broader movement towards African socialism and political unity championed by Nyerere.

The Zanzibar Revolution also had regional implications, as it inspired other liberation movements in Africa. The revolutionaries' success in overthrowing a long-standing Arab-dominated regime resonated with those struggling against colonial and oppressive rule elsewhere on the continent. The revolution served as a beacon of hope and a symbol of the power of popular resistance.

However, the revolution was not without its challenges and complexities. The expulsion of minority communities and the radical policies implemented by the new government led to social and economic disruptions. Zanzibar experienced a period of political instability and economic decline in the aftermath of the revolution, which required significant efforts to rebuild and stabilize the society.

In conclusion, the Zanzibar Revolution of 1964 marked a turning point in the history of Zanzibar and had far-reaching consequences for Tanzania as a whole. The revolutionaries' overthrow of the Sultanate and the establishment of a new government symbolized the aspirations of the African majority for self-determination and social justice. The revolution remains a significant event in Tanzanian history, reminding us of the power of popular resistance and the complexities of post-revolutionary transitions.

The United Republic of Tanzania: Merging Tanganyika and Zanzibar

The establishment of the United Republic of Tanzania in 1964 marked a historic moment in Tanzanian history. This chapter delves into the merger of Tanganyika and Zanzibar, exploring the factors that led to the formation of the united nation and the challenges and achievements that have shaped the country since its inception.

The merger of Tanganyika and Zanzibar was a result of political developments in both regions. Tanganyika, which had gained independence from British colonial rule in 1961, was led by Julius Nyerere and the Tanganyika African National Union (TANU). Zanzibar, following the Zanzibar Revolution of 1964, had established the People's Republic of Zanzibar under the leadership of Abeid Karume and the Afro-Shirazi Party (ASP).

The leaders of Tanganyika and Zanzibar recognized the common goals and shared aspirations of their respective regions. They understood that unity would be a driving force in overcoming the challenges faced by their newly independent nations. Negotiations for the merger began, and on April 26, 1964, Tanganyika and Zanzibar officially merged to form the United Republic of Tanzania.

The merger aimed to create a united and inclusive nation, bringing together the diverse cultures, ethnicities, and histories of Tanganyika and Zanzibar. The union sought to transcend regional divisions and promote national unity, fostering a sense of Tanzanian identity that encompassed both mainland and archipelago.

The United Republic of Tanzania adopted a unique political structure, with two semi-autonomous governments. Tanganyika maintained its own government, led by President Julius Nyerere, while Zanzibar retained its own president and government. The union was guided by the principles of equality, mutual respect, and cooperation, ensuring that both regions had representation and a voice in the governance of the country.

The merger of Tanganyika and Zanzibar presented numerous challenges, including reconciling differences in political ideologies, administrative systems, and socio-economic conditions. However, the leadership of Nyerere and Karume, along with their commitment to unity and progress, helped overcome these challenges and fostered a spirit of cooperation and nation-building.

The United Republic of Tanzania embarked on a path of nation-building and development, guided by the principles of African socialism and self-reliance. Nyerere's philosophy of Ujamaa, which emphasized collective responsibility and rural development, became a guiding framework for Tanzania's socio-economic policies.

The united nation faced significant economic hurdles, including limited resources and structural imbalances. Tanzania implemented policies aimed at industrialization, land reform, and the promotion of self-sufficiency in agriculture. The country also embarked on a program of nationalization, aiming to redistribute wealth and create a more equitable society.

The United Republic of Tanzania played an influential role in regional and international affairs. Under Nyerere's leadership, Tanzania championed Pan-Africanism and supported liberation movements across the continent, providing refuge, training, and diplomatic support to freedom fighters. Tanzania's commitment to peace, justice, and anti-imperialism earned the country a respected place in the global community.

The United Republic of Tanzania faced its share of challenges, including political tensions, economic setbacks, and the complexities of managing a diverse and geographically vast nation. However, the country also celebrated significant achievements. Tanzania made strides in education, healthcare, and social welfare, striving to uplift its citizens and build a more equitable society.

In recent years, Tanzania has experienced political transitions and shifts in policy, reflecting the changing dynamics of the country. The legacy of the united republic remains, as Tanzania continues to navigate the complexities of governance, economic development, and social progress.

In conclusion, the merger of Tanganyika and Zanzibar to form the United Republic of Tanzania symbolized a remarkable moment in Tanzanian history. The union sought to forge a united nation, transcending regional and ethnic divisions. Tanzania's journey as a united republic has been marked by challenges, achievements, and ongoing efforts to build a vibrant and inclusive society. The united republic stands as a testament to the power of unity, cooperation, and the pursuit of a shared national vision.

Ujamaa: Nyerere's Vision for Socialism and Self-Reliance

Julius Nyerere, the founding father of Tanzania, had a profound vision for the country's socio-economic development. Central to his philosophy was the concept of Ujamaa, which emphasized socialism, self-reliance, and communal values. This chapter explores Nyerere's vision for Ujamaa, its implementation in Tanzania, and its lasting impact on the nation's trajectory.

Nyerere's vision for Ujamaa emerged from his deep commitment to addressing the inequalities and injustices inherited from the colonial era. He sought to establish a society rooted in African values, where individuals worked collectively for the common good and everyone had access to basic needs, such as education, healthcare, and housing.

The Ujamaa philosophy drew inspiration from Tanzania's cultural heritage, particularly communal practices prevalent in rural areas. Nyerere envisioned a society where Tanzanians would live in self-sustaining villages, practicing communal farming and sharing resources. This model aimed to promote equitable distribution of wealth, foster social cohesion, and empower local communities.

The implementation of Ujamaa in Tanzania began with the Arusha Declaration of 1967. This declaration outlined the principles and goals of Ujamaa, calling for the nationalization of land, the creation of cooperative farms, and the development of rural industries. The Arusha Declaration signaled a radical departure from the capitalist model and set Tanzania on a path of socialist transformation.

One of the key objectives of Ujamaa was to achieve economic self-reliance. Nyerere recognized the detrimental effects of dependency on foreign aid and sought to build a self-sufficient nation. Tanzania implemented policies to promote import substitution, industrialization, and the development of local industries. The focus was on utilizing domestic resources, improving agricultural productivity, and reducing reliance on foreign imports.

The Ujamaa approach also emphasized education as a catalyst for social progress. Nyerere believed that an educated population was essential for the success of Ujamaa and the overall development of Tanzania. The government invested heavily in expanding access to education, building schools, and training teachers. Education became a cornerstone of social mobility and empowerment.

The implementation of Ujamaa was not without challenges. The transition from individual land ownership to communal ownership faced resistance and required significant adjustments. The cooperative farming model, although designed to promote collective ownership and equal distribution, faced difficulties in terms of productivity and incentives for individual effort. The ambitious goals of self-reliance also encountered obstacles, including limited resources, inadequate infrastructure, and global economic pressures.

Despite these challenges, Ujamaa left a lasting impact on Tanzania. The philosophy fostered a sense of national unity, as Tanzanians worked together towards shared goals.

Ujamaa instilled a spirit of self-reliance, encouraging Tanzanians to tap into their own resources and capabilities to overcome obstacles. The focus on education and social welfare led to improvements in literacy rates, healthcare access, and living standards.

Nyerere's leadership and commitment to Ujamaa garnered international recognition. Tanzania became a model for other African nations pursuing socialist development and self-reliance. Nyerere's voice carried weight in international forums, as he advocated for global justice, anti-imperialism, and the rights of developing nations.

In the 1980s, Tanzania underwent economic reforms that shifted its trajectory away from the Ujamaa model. The country embraced market-oriented policies, privatization, and structural adjustments in response to global economic trends. The legacy of Ujamaa, however, remains embedded in Tanzanian society and continues to shape the country's development priorities.

In conclusion, Ujamaa represented Nyerere's visionary approach to nation-building in Tanzania. The philosophy emphasized socialism, self-reliance, and communal values, seeking to address historical injustices and foster an equitable society. Although the implementation of Ujamaa faced challenges, it left a profound impact on Tanzania's socio-economic landscape, fostering a spirit of unity, self-sufficiency, and social progress. The legacy of Ujamaa endures as Tanzania navigates the complexities of modern development, drawing inspiration from the ideals of collective responsibility and shared prosperity.

The Arusha Declaration: Tanzania's Commitment to Equality and Development

The Arusha Declaration of 1967 stands as a seminal moment in Tanzania's history, representing the country's commitment to social equality, economic development, and self-reliance. This chapter delves into the Arusha Declaration, exploring its origins, objectives, and impact on Tanzania's socio-economic landscape.

The Arusha Declaration was a comprehensive policy statement unveiled by President Julius Nyerere on February 5, 1967, in the city of Arusha, Tanzania. The declaration outlined the principles and goals of Tanzania's socialist transformation and provided a roadmap for the country's development trajectory.

At its core, the Arusha Declaration aimed to address the deep-rooted inequalities inherited from colonial rule and create a more just and equitable society. It called for the nationalization of land and natural resources, the establishment of cooperative farms, and the promotion of rural industries. The declaration emphasized the need for collective ownership, communal values, and shared benefits.

One of the central tenets of the Arusha Declaration was the commitment to equality. Nyerere recognized the disparities that existed within Tanzanian society and sought to bridge the gap between the privileged few and the majority who lived in poverty. The declaration emphasized the redistribution of wealth, access to education and healthcare, and the elimination of discrimination based on race, gender, or social status.

The Arusha Declaration highlighted the importance of self-reliance as a means to achieve sustainable development. Tanzania aimed to reduce dependency on foreign aid and imports by tapping into its own resources and capabilities. The declaration encouraged industrialization, import substitution, and the promotion of local industries to boost economic growth and reduce reliance on external factors.

The implementation of the Arusha Declaration was a complex and multifaceted process. The nationalization of land and industries required careful planning and coordination, as well as the mobilization of resources and human capital. The establishment of cooperative farms sought to empower local communities, increase agricultural productivity, and ensure food security.

The Arusha Declaration also emphasized the importance of education as a catalyst for development. Nyerere believed that education was the key to social mobility and empowerment. The declaration called for expanded access to quality education, the training of teachers, and the eradication of illiteracy. Education became a cornerstone of Tanzania's development agenda, enabling individuals to actively contribute to the nation's progress.

The impact of the Arusha Declaration was significant. It set Tanzania on a path of socialist transformation and self-reliance, emphasizing the principles of social justice, equality, and collective responsibility. The declaration instilled a sense of national unity and common purpose, as Tanzanians rallied around the vision of a more equitable and prosperous society.

The Arusha Declaration gained international attention and admiration, as it presented an alternative model of development rooted in African values. Tanzania became a beacon of hope for other developing nations seeking to overcome historical injustices and achieve self-determination. Nyerere's leadership and the Arusha Declaration inspired a generation of leaders across Africa, shaping the discourse on African socialism and development.

Over time, Tanzania underwent economic reforms that shifted its trajectory away from the strict implementation of the Arusha Declaration. The country embraced market-oriented policies and structural adjustments in response to changing global trends. However, the spirit and principles of the declaration continue to influence Tanzania's development policies and the pursuit of social justice.

In conclusion, the Arusha Declaration represented Tanzania's commitment to equality and development. It served as a roadmap for the country's socialist transformation, emphasizing social justice, self-reliance, and collective responsibility. The declaration left a lasting impact on Tanzania's socio-economic landscape, shaping the pursuit of a more equitable society and fostering a sense of national unity and purpose. The ideals of the Arusha Declaration continue to resonate as Tanzania strives for inclusive and sustainable development.

The Liberation Struggle: Tanzania's Support for Southern African Independence

Tanzania played a pivotal role in the liberation struggle of Southern Africa, providing unwavering support to movements fighting against colonialism, apartheid, and oppression. This chapter explores Tanzania's significant contributions to the liberation efforts, showcasing its commitment to Pan-Africanism, solidarity, and the pursuit of freedom in the region.

Tanzania's involvement in the liberation struggle stemmed from President Julius Nyerere's firm belief in the principles of self-determination, justice, and equality. Nyerere recognized that the struggle against colonial rule and apartheid in Southern Africa was not isolated but intertwined with the broader fight for freedom and human rights across the continent.

One of the most notable examples of Tanzania's support for Southern African independence was its assistance to the African National Congress (ANC) in South Africa. Tanzania provided a safe haven and logistical support to ANC leaders and activists who sought refuge from the apartheid regime. The ANC established its headquarters in Tanzania, utilizing the country as a base for operations, training, and diplomatic efforts.

Tanzania also supported other liberation movements in the region, including the Zimbabwe African National Union (ZANU) and the South West African People's Organization (SWAPO). Nyerere's government provided training camps, military assistance, and diplomatic backing to these movements, aiding their struggle for independence from colonial powers.

The support extended beyond military and diplomatic aid. Tanzania welcomed exiled students and activists from Southern Africa, offering them educational opportunities and a platform to advocate for their respective causes. These individuals played a crucial role in raising awareness about the plight of their nations and garnering international support for the liberation struggle.

Tanzania hosted numerous conferences and meetings, providing a platform for dialogue and coordination among the various liberation movements. The country became a hub for Pan-Africanist solidarity, as leaders from across the continent gathered to strategize, exchange ideas, and strengthen their resolve in the face of oppression.

Tanzania's commitment to the liberation struggle was not without risks and sacrifices. The government faced threats, diplomatic pressures, and even military incursions from neighboring countries. However, Tanzania stood firm in its principles, undeterred by the challenges, and remained a steadfast supporter of Southern African independence.

The efforts of Tanzania and its contributions to the liberation struggle were not in vain. The perseverance and resilience of the liberation movements, combined with international pressure and solidarity, ultimately led to the dismantling of apartheid and the independence of nations such as Zimbabwe, Namibia, and South Africa.

Tanzania's role in the liberation struggle garnered international recognition and admiration. President

Nyerere's moral leadership and his unwavering commitment to justice and freedom resonated with leaders and activists worldwide. Tanzania became a symbol of hope and inspiration, inspiring other nations and individuals to stand up against oppression and fight for their rights.

The impact of Tanzania's support for Southern African independence extended beyond political boundaries. It strengthened regional cooperation, fostered a sense of Pan-African unity, and established enduring bonds of friendship among nations. Tanzania's contributions to the liberation struggle remain a significant part of its legacy, highlighting the country's commitment to justice, freedom, and the principles of Pan-Africanism.

In conclusion, Tanzania's support for Southern African independence represented a shining example of solidarity and commitment to the liberation struggle. Through its aid to liberation movements, hosting conferences, and providing refuge to activists, Tanzania played a vital role in the dismantling of colonialism and apartheid in the region. The country's contributions left an indelible mark on the path to freedom and inspired generations to continue the fight for justice and equality.

Natural Treasures: Wildlife Conservation in Tanzania

Tanzania is renowned for its remarkable natural treasures and abundant wildlife. This chapter delves into the country's commitment to wildlife conservation, exploring its diverse ecosystems, iconic species, conservation efforts, and the importance of preserving Tanzania's natural heritage for future generations.

Tanzania boasts a wealth of diverse ecosystems, ranging from the vast Serengeti plains to the magnificent Mount Kilimanjaro, from the stunning Ngorongoro Crater to the picturesque Zanzibar Archipelago. These diverse landscapes support a wide array of flora and fauna, making Tanzania a paradise for wildlife enthusiasts and nature lovers.

One of Tanzania's most iconic and celebrated wildlife phenomena is the Great Wildebeest Migration, an awe-inspiring annual event that sees millions of wildebeest, zebras, and other herbivores journeying across the Serengeti in search of fresh grazing. This natural spectacle is not only a breathtaking sight but also a testament to the importance of preserving the habitats and migration routes that sustain these incredible animal populations.

Tanzania is home to a rich variety of wildlife, including the Big Five (elephant, lion, leopard, buffalo, and rhinoceros). Other iconic species that roam the country's national parks and reserves include giraffes, cheetahs, zebras, hyenas, hippos, crocodiles, and numerous bird species. The vast array of wildlife attracts tourists from around the world, contributing to Tanzania's economy and fostering an appreciation for conservation.

Recognizing the value of its natural heritage, Tanzania has made significant efforts to conserve its wildlife and protect its ecosystems. The government, in collaboration with local communities and international partners, has established an extensive network of national parks, game reserves, and conservation areas. These protected areas serve as sanctuaries for wildlife, enabling them to thrive and ensuring their long-term survival.

One of Tanzania's most famous conservation success stories is the establishment of the Serengeti National Park. This UNESCO World Heritage Site spans an area of over 14,750 square kilometers and provides a safe haven for a vast array of species, including the largest population of lions in Africa. Efforts to protect the Serengeti's unique ecosystems and wildlife have been instrumental in maintaining its ecological balance and preserving its extraordinary biodiversity.

Tanzania has also taken proactive measures to combat poaching and illegal wildlife trafficking, recognizing the devastating impact these activities have on endangered species such as elephants and rhinoceroses. The government has implemented stringent anti-poaching measures, increased law enforcement efforts, and collaborated with international organizations to tackle this critical issue. These initiatives aim to safeguard Tanzania's wildlife heritage for future generations.

Furthermore, Tanzania is actively involved in community-based conservation initiatives, recognizing the importance of engaging local communities in conservation efforts. By involving communities in wildlife management and providing them with alternative livelihood opportunities, Tanzania promotes a sustainable approach to conservation that benefits both people and wildlife. These initiatives not only foster a sense of ownership and responsibility but also contribute to poverty alleviation and the preservation of cultural heritage.

Tanzania's commitment to wildlife conservation extends beyond its borders. The country is a signatory to international agreements and conventions aimed at protecting endangered species and their habitats. Tanzania's participation in initiatives such as the Convention on International Trade in Endangered Species of Wild Fauna and Flora (CITES) reflects its dedication to global conservation efforts and cooperation.

In conclusion, Tanzania's dedication to wildlife conservation is evident in its diverse ecosystems, iconic species, and comprehensive conservation strategies. The country's efforts to protect its natural treasures, combat poaching, engage local communities, and participate in international conservation initiatives showcase its commitment to preserving its wildlife heritage. By safeguarding Tanzania's natural wonders, the nation contributes not only to the well-being of its own people but also to the global community's understanding and appreciation of nature's beauty and importance.

The Serengeti: A Journey through the African Savannah

The Serengeti is an iconic and captivating landscape, often described as the crown jewel of Tanzania's natural wonders. This chapter takes readers on a virtual journey through the African savannah, exploring the unique features, diverse wildlife, and the significance of the Serengeti ecosystem.

The Serengeti, located in northern Tanzania, spans an impressive area of approximately 30,000 square kilometers. It forms part of the larger Serengeti-Mara ecosystem, which extends into Kenya's Maasai Mara National Reserve. The name "Serengeti" originates from the Maasai language, meaning "endless plains," a fitting description for the vast stretches of grasslands that define the region.

The Serengeti's most famous natural spectacle is undoubtedly the Great Wildebeest Migration, a breathtaking phenomenon that involves millions of wildebeest, zebras, and other herbivores undertaking a perilous journey in search of fresh grazing. This remarkable event is driven by the availability of food and water, as the animals move in a cyclical pattern following the rainfall and the growth of grass.

The migration starts in the southern Serengeti, usually around December or January, when the herds gather to give birth to their young during the calving season. As the dry season progresses, the herds begin their northward trek, crossing rivers teeming with crocodiles and facing other challenges such as predation and exhaustion. The migration reaches its climax around July, when the herds attempt to cross the Mara River and continue into the Maasai Mara in Kenya.

The Serengeti is not solely about the migration. It hosts an incredibly diverse array of wildlife throughout the year. The region is renowned for its large populations of lions, leopards, elephants, and buffalos, which are collectively known as the "Big Five." Cheetahs, hyenas, giraffes, zebras, hippos, and numerous antelope species also call the Serengeti home. Bird enthusiasts will delight in the more than 500 bird species found within the ecosystem.

The Serengeti's diverse habitats contribute to its remarkable biodiversity. The ecosystem comprises a mosaic of grassy plains, woodland areas, rocky outcrops known as kopjes, and riverine forests. Each habitat supports different species and offers distinct ecological niches. The open plains provide prime grazing grounds for herbivores, while the woodlands and riverbanks offer shelter and sustenance for predators.

The Serengeti is not just a wildlife haven; it also plays a crucial role in the conservation of biodiversity. The region is protected as the Serengeti National Park, which was established in 1951 and later designated as a UNESCO World Heritage Site. The park, together with adjacent conservation areas and reserves, safeguards the delicate balance of the ecosystem and ensures the long-term survival of its inhabitants.

Beyond its ecological significance, the Serengeti holds cultural and historical importance. The Maasai people have inhabited the region for centuries and maintain a deep connection to the land and its wildlife. Their traditional pastoralist lifestyle has coexisted harmoniously with the wildlife, and their rich cultural heritage adds another layer of intrigue to the Serengeti experience.

Exploring the Serengeti is a captivating adventure that offers diverse experiences. Visitors can embark on game drives, guided walking safaris, or even hot air balloon rides to witness the wildlife and the breathtaking landscapes from different perspectives. The annual migration is undoubtedly a highlight, but even outside of migration season, the Serengeti's wildlife, stunning sunsets, and vast plains provide a feast for the senses.

Preserving the Serengeti and ensuring its sustainability is a shared responsibility. Efforts are in place to combat poaching, manage tourism, and engage local communities in conservation initiatives. Sustainable tourism practices, such as responsible guiding and low-impact accommodations, help minimize the ecological footprint and preserve the natural integrity of the ecosystem.

In conclusion, the Serengeti is a mesmerizing destination that encapsulates the awe-inspiring beauty and biodiversity of the African savannah. Its remarkable wildlife, stunning landscapes, and the annual Great Wildebeest Migration make it a bucket-list experience for nature enthusiasts and wildlife lovers. The Serengeti's conservation efforts, combined with responsible tourism practices, aim to safeguard this precious ecosystem for generations to come, ensuring that the journey through the African savannah continues to captivate and inspire all who visit.

Ngorongoro Crater: Exploring the World's Largest Unbroken Caldera

Nestled in the heart of Tanzania's northern circuit, the Ngorongoro Crater is a natural wonder that beckons visitors from around the world. This chapter invites readers to embark on an exploration of the world's largest unbroken caldera, delving into its geological origins, unique ecosystem, and the unforgettable experiences it offers.

The Ngorongoro Crater is a massive volcanic caldera that formed millions of years ago. It stretches over an area of approximately 260 square kilometers and reaches a depth of about 610 meters. This geological marvel was created by the collapse of a large volcano, resulting in a sunken bowl-shaped depression that now encompasses a diverse range of habitats and a wealth of wildlife.

The crater's diverse ecosystem is a testament to its geological history and the protection it provides to its inhabitants. The walls of the caldera act as a natural barrier, enclosing an astonishing array of wildlife within its boundaries. From lush grasslands to acacia woodlands, from soda lakes to fever tree forests, the Ngorongoro Crater offers a mosaic of habitats that sustain an abundance of species.

One of the highlights of the Ngorongoro Crater is its thriving population of wildlife. The crater is home to an estimated 25,000 large animals, including elephants, buffalos, zebras, wildebeests, and gazelles. The dense concentration of herbivores attracts an equally impressive predator population, including lions, leopards, cheetahs, and hyenas. The crater's relatively confined space makes wildlife encounters almost inevitable, creating a remarkable opportunity for visitors to observe these magnificent creatures up close.

The Ngorongoro Crater is also a haven for bird enthusiasts, with over 500 bird species recorded in the area. From flamingos congregating in the soda lakes to eagles soaring in the sky, the crater's diverse birdlife adds a splash of color and melody to the already captivating scenery.

Exploring the Ngorongoro Crater is an adventure that takes visitors on a journey through its varied landscapes and wildlife-rich territories. Game drives are the most common way to experience the crater's wonders, offering the opportunity to traverse the crater floor and witness the intricate web of life unfold before your eyes. Experienced guides navigate the terrain, sharing their knowledge and insights, ensuring an informative and unforgettable safari experience.

One of the unique aspects of the Ngorongoro Crater is its coexistence of wildlife and Maasai communities. The Maasai people, known for their traditional semi-nomadic lifestyle, have inhabited the region for centuries. Their harmonious relationship with the wildlife and the land adds a cultural dimension to the Ngorongoro experience. Some Maasai villages offer visitors a glimpse into their daily lives, allowing for a deeper understanding of their customs, traditions, and connection to the natural world.

Preserving the delicate balance of the Ngorongoro Crater is of utmost importance. The area is designated as a conservation area and is recognized as a UNESCO World Heritage Site. Strict regulations are in place to ensure sustainable tourism practices, such as limiting the number of vehicles and adhering to designated routes. These measures help minimize the impact on the ecosystem and ensure the long-term conservation of this extraordinary natural treasure.

Visiting the Ngorongoro Crater is a journey that leaves a lasting impression. The sheer scale and beauty of the caldera, coupled with the abundance of wildlife and the fascinating coexistence of nature and culture, create a truly unforgettable experience. Whether it's witnessing a lioness hunting her prey, marveling at the stunning views from the crater rim, or immersing oneself in the rich Maasai heritage, the Ngorongoro Crater captivates the senses and leaves visitors with a deep appreciation for the wonders of the natural world.

In conclusion, the Ngorongoro Crater is a testament to the Earth's geological history and the intricate balance of nature. Its size, unique ecosystem, and concentration of wildlife make it a must-visit destination for wildlife enthusiasts and nature lovers. The preservation of this remarkable caldera ensures that future generations can continue to explore, admire, and be inspired by the world's largest unbroken caldera, forever cherishing its awe-inspiring beauty and the incredible biodiversity it supports.

Spice Islands: Zanzibar's Fragrant Legacy

Zanzibar, often referred to as the "Spice Islands," is a captivating archipelago off the coast of Tanzania, renowned for its rich history, vibrant culture, and, of course, its fragrant spice trade. This chapter delves into the legacy of Zanzibar as a spice hub, exploring its aromatic treasures, historical significance, and the enduring impact of the spice industry.

For centuries, Zanzibar has been synonymous with the spice trade, attracting traders and explorers from around the world in search of its prized aromatic treasures. The islands' strategic location in the Indian Ocean made them a crossroads for maritime trade routes, facilitating the exchange of goods, cultures, and ideas.

Zanzibar's tropical climate, fertile soil, and abundant rainfall create the perfect conditions for growing a wide array of spices. The archipelago is home to various spice plantations, where cloves, nutmeg, cinnamon, pepper, cardamom, and vanilla thrive. These spices not only add flavor and fragrance to culinary creations but also possess medicinal and cultural significance.

Cloves, in particular, have played a crucial role in Zanzibar's history and economy. Zanzibar was once the world's leading producer of cloves, accounting for a significant portion of global production. The archipelago's cloves were highly sought after, with merchants from Europe, Arabia, and beyond flocking to Zanzibar to acquire these aromatic buds.

The spice trade brought immense wealth and cultural exchange to Zanzibar. Arab, Persian, Indian, and European merchants established trading posts and settlements on the islands, leaving a lasting impact on the archipelago's architecture, cuisine, and cultural traditions. Zanzibar became a melting pot of diverse influences, resulting in a unique blend of African, Arabian, and Indian cultures.

Zanzibar's capital city, Stone Town, is a UNESCO World Heritage Site and a testament to the archipelago's rich history. Its narrow winding streets, intricately carved doors, and bustling markets evoke a sense of the past, where the scent of spices lingers in the air. Exploring the spice markets of Stone Town is an immersive experience that tantalizes the senses and offers a glimpse into Zanzibar's fragrant legacy.

The spice industry continues to be an integral part of Zanzibar's economy and cultural identity. Spice tours provide visitors with an opportunity to learn about the cultivation, processing, and uses of various spices. Guided tours take visitors through lush plantations, where they can see firsthand how cloves, vanilla, and other spices are grown and harvested. They can also witness traditional spice processing techniques, such as drying and grinding, and even participate in spice-infused cooking demonstrations.

Zanzibar's spice heritage extends beyond its culinary and cultural significance. The islands' spices have medicinal properties and are used in traditional healing practices. Cloves, for instance, are believed to have analgesic and antiseptic properties and are often used to alleviate toothaches and digestive ailments. The aromatic spices of

Zanzibar are also key ingredients in traditional perfumes, soaps, and beauty products.

The legacy of Zanzibar's spice trade can be seen and tasted in its vibrant cuisine. The aromatic spices infuse Zanzibari dishes with unique flavors and aromas. From the tantalizing blend of spices in pilau rice to the zesty kick of the Zanzibari curry known as "biryani," the archipelago's culinary offerings are a testament to the enduring influence of the spice trade.

In recent years, Zanzibar has embraced its spice heritage as a tourist attraction, offering visitors the opportunity to explore the spice plantations, engage with local communities, and learn about the history and significance of each spice. This sustainable approach to tourism allows visitors to support local farmers and communities while experiencing the fragrant legacy of Zanzibar firsthand.

In conclusion, Zanzibar's designation as the "Spice Islands" is a testament to its aromatic treasures and the enduring legacy of the spice trade. The archipelago's strategic location, fertile soil, and vibrant cultural exchange have made it a hub for the production and trade of aromatic spices. Zanzibar's spice industry has shaped its history, culture, cuisine, and economy, leaving an indelible mark on the archipelago's identity. Exploring Zanzibar's fragrant legacy offers a captivating journey through time, immersing visitors in the scents, tastes, and stories that continue to enchant all who visit the Spice Islands.

Dar es Salaam: From Fishing Village to Modern Metropolis

Dar es Salaam, Tanzania's largest city and economic hub, has a fascinating history that spans centuries. This chapter traces the evolution of Dar es Salaam from a humble fishing village to a bustling modern metropolis, highlighting its historical milestones, cultural diversity, and the remarkable growth that has shaped its identity.

The origins of Dar es Salaam can be traced back to the 19th century when it was a small fishing village inhabited by the indigenous Zaramo people. The location, situated along the coast of the Indian Ocean, made it an ideal trading post for Arab and Swahili traders, who established settlements and engaged in commerce with the local communities.

The name "Dar es Salaam" translates to "Haven of Peace" in Arabic, reflecting the city's early reputation as a tranquil and harmonious trading center. The town grew gradually as it attracted merchants, sailors, and explorers from various parts of the world, drawn to its strategic position on the East African coast.

In the late 19th century, Dar es Salaam came under German colonial rule when the German East Africa Company established a presence in the region. The Germans recognized the strategic importance of the city and developed it as a major port and administrative center. Infrastructure projects, including the construction of a railway line connecting Dar es Salaam to the interior, brought about significant development and contributed to its growth as a regional trade hub.

During the early 20th century, Dar es Salaam continued to flourish under German rule. The city's population increased, and its economic significance expanded, attracting traders, plantation owners, and entrepreneurs. The Germans left a lasting architectural imprint on the city, evident in the colonial buildings and structures that still grace its streets today.

After World War I, Dar es Salaam came under British rule as part of the Tanganyika territory. Under British administration, the city experienced further development and urbanization. Investments in infrastructure, education, and healthcare improved the quality of life for its residents and stimulated economic growth.

The process of decolonization in Africa led to Tanzania gaining independence in 1961. Dar es Salaam became the capital of the newly formed country, taking on a pivotal role in shaping the nation's political, economic, and cultural landscape. The city underwent rapid urbanization and transformation as it accommodated the influx of people and became the center of government institutions, diplomatic missions, and commercial activities.

Dar es Salaam's growth continued in the post-independence era, fueled by its strategic location and the opportunities it offered. The city became a major port, handling international trade and connecting Tanzania to the global market. Industries such as manufacturing, finance, telecommunications, and tourism flourished, contributing to the city's economic vitality.

Today, Dar es Salaam stands as a vibrant metropolis with a diverse population and a thriving urban culture. The city's skyline is dotted with modern skyscrapers, shopping malls, and bustling markets. Its streets are filled with a blend of traditional and contemporary architecture, reflecting the fusion of cultures that have shaped its identity.

Dar es Salaam is a melting pot of different ethnicities, languages, and religions. The city's cosmopolitan nature is evident in its diverse neighborhoods, where people from various backgrounds coexist and contribute to the social fabric. This cultural diversity is reflected in the vibrant arts, music, cuisine, and festivals that define the city's cultural scene.

Efforts have been made to enhance the city's infrastructure and improve the quality of life for its residents. Expansion projects, including the construction of new roads, bridges, and public transportation systems, aim to address the challenges of urbanization and support sustainable growth. The city is also investing in education, healthcare, and social services to meet the needs of its expanding population.

In conclusion, Dar es Salaam's journey from a humble fishing village to a modern metropolis is a testament to Tanzania's progress and urban development. Its strategic coastal location, historical significance, and cultural diversity have shaped its growth and influenced its identity. Today, Dar es Salaam stands as a dynamic city, embodying the spirit of Tanzania's ambition, resilience, and multicultural heritage.

Stone Town: Tracing the History of Zanzibar's Cultural Gem

Stone Town, the historic heart of Zanzibar City, is a captivating UNESCO World Heritage Site that offers a glimpse into the rich history, cultural diversity, and architectural wonders of Zanzibar. This chapter takes readers on a journey through time, tracing the history of Stone Town and uncovering the layers of its cultural gem.

Stone Town's roots can be traced back to the 9th century when Arab traders established a trading post on the island of Zanzibar, drawn by its strategic location along the Indian Ocean trade routes. Over the centuries, the settlement grew in size and importance, attracting merchants, explorers, and settlers from Africa, Arabia, Persia, India, and Europe.

The name "Stone Town" aptly describes the city's unique architecture, characterized by intricately carved coral stone buildings that line its narrow winding streets. The use of coral stone, a prevalent building material in Zanzibar, not only lends the town its distinctive charm but also reflects the island's geological heritage.

Stone Town's architecture is a fusion of different influences, reflecting the diverse cultural and historical layers that have shaped Zanzibar's identity. Arab, Persian, Indian, and European architectural styles blend seamlessly, resulting in a captivating blend of Swahili, Islamic, and colonial influences.

One of the most prominent architectural features of Stone Town is its ornately carved wooden doors. These doors are true works of art, with intricate designs and motifs that tell stories of the families and cultures that reside behind them. Each door is unique, reflecting the status, wealth, and heritage of the occupants.

Exploring Stone Town is like stepping back in time. The city's narrow streets, known as "mitaa," are a labyrinth of history, leading visitors through bustling markets, hidden courtyards, and vibrant squares. The maze-like layout of the streets served as a defense mechanism against invaders, creating a complex network that adds to the charm and intrigue of the town.

Stone Town's historical significance goes beyond its architectural splendor. The city played a pivotal role in the Indian Ocean trade network, serving as a hub for the exchange of goods, cultures, and ideas. Its thriving markets attracted traders from far and wide, creating a cosmopolitan atmosphere that lingers to this day.

One of the notable landmarks in Stone Town is the Old Fort, also known as Ngome Kongwe. Built by the Omani Arabs in the 17th century, the fort served as a defensive structure and later became a prison. Today, it stands as a cultural center, hosting exhibitions, events, and a popular open-air amphitheater where performances take place.

Another iconic site in Stone Town is the House of Wonders, locally known as Beit-al-Ajaib. This grand palace, constructed in the late 19th century, was one of the first buildings in East Africa to have electricity and an elevator. It now houses the Museum of History and Culture of Zanzibar and the Swahili Coast, providing visitors with insights into the island's past.

The Forodhani Gardens, located along the waterfront, offer a respite from the bustling streets of Stone Town. This popular gathering place comes alive in the evenings with food stalls offering an array of Zanzibari delights, including freshly grilled seafood, Zanzibar pizza, and tropical fruits. It's a vibrant and sensory experience that showcases the island's culinary heritage.

Stone Town is also home to several mosques, including the iconic Beit-al-Ajaib Mosque and the Old Slave Market Mosque, which stands as a somber reminder of Zanzibar's dark history of the slave trade. The Anglican Cathedral, built on the site of the former slave market, stands as a symbol of reconciliation and commemorates the abolition of the slave trade.

Preserving Stone Town's unique heritage is of paramount importance. Efforts have been made to restore and maintain the town's historical buildings, with organizations and stakeholders working together to ensure the conservation and sustainable development of this cultural gem. Strict regulations are in place to protect the architectural integrity of Stone Town and maintain its status as a UNESCO World Heritage Site.

In conclusion, Stone Town is a cultural gem that encapsulates the rich history, architectural splendor, and vibrant heritage of Zanzibar. Its labyrinthine streets, ornate doors, and fusion of cultural influences create a captivating tapestry that reflects the island's past and present. Exploring Stone Town is an immersive experience that allows visitors to trace the footsteps of traders, scholars, and explorers, and appreciate the enduring legacy of this remarkable cultural gem.

Bagamoyo: A Portal to the Past and Slave Trade Heritage

Bagamoyo, a small coastal town in Tanzania, holds a significant place in the country's history as a portal to the past and a poignant reminder of the dark legacy of the slave trade. This chapter delves into the rich historical tapestry of Bagamoyo, exploring its role as a center of trade, its connection to the slave trade, and the efforts to preserve its heritage.

Bagamoyo's name translates to "lay down your heart" in Swahili, a reflection of its deep historical and emotional significance. The town's location along the coast of the Indian Ocean made it an important trading port and a gateway to the interior of East Africa. Arab and Swahili traders established settlements in Bagamoyo, creating a cosmopolitan atmosphere that attracted merchants, explorers, and missionaries.

During the 19th century, Bagamoyo became a major hub of the East African slave trade. The town served as a key transit point, where enslaved Africans were captured, held, and subsequently transported to various parts of the world. The painful memory of this dark chapter in history is still palpable in Bagamoyo today.

The remnants of Bagamoyo's slave trade past can be explored through various historical sites. The Bagamoyo Slave Route, a UNESCO World Heritage Site, traces the path that enslaved individuals were forced to walk from the interior to the coast. This trail serves as a poignant reminder of the suffering and resilience of those who endured the horrors of the slave trade.

One of the notable landmarks in Bagamoyo is the Kaole Ruins. These ruins, dating back to the 13th century, offer a glimpse into the town's pre-colonial past. They include the remains of mosques, tombs, and other structures, providing insights into the architectural and cultural heritage of the region.

Bagamoyo's historical significance extends beyond the slave trade. The town was a center of exploration and missionary activity during the 19th century. It was from Bagamoyo that renowned explorers such as Richard Burton, John Hanning Speke, and Henry Morton Stanley embarked on their journeys into the interior of Africa.

Bagamoyo also played a pivotal role in the Arab-Swahili trade network. The town was a bustling center for the exchange of goods, including ivory, spices, timber, and other commodities. The vibrant markets, ancient dhows, and historical buildings that line the streets offer glimpses into the town's mercantile past.

Efforts have been made to preserve Bagamoyo's historical and cultural heritage. The Bagamoyo Arts and Cultural Institute, established in 1986, promotes the preservation and celebration of traditional Tanzanian arts, music, and dance. The institute offers workshops and performances that provide insights into the region's rich cultural traditions.

Bagamoyo is also home to the Bagamoyo College of Arts, a renowned institution that offers training in various artistic disciplines. The college serves as a hub for nurturing local talent and preserving traditional artistic practices, contributing to the cultural vibrancy of the town.

Visiting Bagamoyo is a journey that invites reflection and contemplation. The town's historical sites, museums, and exhibitions provide opportunities to learn about the complexities of its past and the resilience of its people. The Bagamoyo Festival of Arts and Culture, held annually, showcases the region's artistic heritage and serves as a platform for cultural exchange and dialogue.

Bagamoyo's historical significance and its connection to the slave trade make it an important destination for heritage tourism. Visitors have the opportunity to engage with the local community, explore the historical sites, and contribute to ongoing efforts to preserve and promote Bagamoyo's cultural legacy.

In conclusion, Bagamoyo stands as a portal to the past, bearing witness to the complex layers of history and the enduring legacy of the slave trade. It serves as a reminder of the atrocities committed during that era, while also embracing the richness of Tanzanian culture and the resilience of its people. Exploring Bagamoyo offers a profound and thought-provoking experience, fostering understanding and encouraging dialogue about the shared history of humanity.

Mwanza: The Gateway to Lake Victoria

Mwanza, situated on the shores of Lake Victoria, holds a special place as the gateway to Africa's largest lake. This chapter explores the captivating city of Mwanza, its historical significance, its connection to Lake Victoria, and the cultural and natural treasures it offers to visitors.

Mwanza is the second-largest city in Tanzania and serves as the economic and cultural hub of the Lake Zone region. The city's name is derived from the Nyamwezi word "Wanza," which means "rocky place," reflecting the rugged terrain and rocky outcrops that characterize the area.

The strategic location of Mwanza on the southern shores of Lake Victoria has contributed to its growth and importance as a transportation and trading hub. The city connects Tanzania to neighboring countries such as Uganda, Kenya, and Rwanda, facilitating cross-border trade and regional integration.

Lake Victoria, known as "Nyanza" in the local Luo language, is the largest freshwater lake in Africa and the second-largest freshwater lake in the world. Mwanza's proximity to this majestic lake has played a significant role in the city's development and cultural identity. The lake provides a livelihood for many local communities, supports a thriving fishing industry, and offers a range of recreational activities.

One of the iconic landmarks in Mwanza is the Bismarck Rock, a massive granite rock formation that juts out into

Lake Victoria. This natural wonder has become a symbol of the city and is a popular spot for visitors to admire panoramic views of the lake and surrounding landscape.

Mwanza's vibrant cultural scene reflects the diversity of its population, which consists of various ethnic groups, including the Sukuma, the largest ethnic group in Tanzania. The Sukuma people have a rich cultural heritage and are known for their traditional music, dance, and vibrant festivals. The city comes alive during cultural events, such as the Bujora Sukuma Museum Festival, where visitors can experience the Sukuma culture through music, dance performances, and traditional arts and crafts.

Mwanza's bustling markets are a vibrant reflection of its trading heritage. The Central Market, locally known as "Soko Kuu," is a hive of activity, offering a variety of fresh produce, textiles, crafts, and other goods. Exploring the market provides a sensory experience, where the sights, sounds, and aromas of local life intertwine.

Lake Victoria offers numerous recreational opportunities for visitors to Mwanza. Boat trips and fishing excursions allow visitors to explore the lake's vast waters, visit nearby islands, and engage in sport fishing. The lake is home to a diverse range of fish species, including the Nile perch, which attracts anglers from around the world.

The city's urban landscape is continually evolving, with new infrastructure developments and modernization projects underway. The Mwanza Port, one of the busiest ports on Lake Victoria, has undergone significant upgrades to enhance its capacity and improve trade links. The city's skyline is changing, with the construction of high-rise buildings, hotels, and shopping centers to cater to the growing demand for tourism and business activities.

Mwanza's natural beauty extends beyond Lake Victoria. The nearby Rubondo Island National Park, located on Rubondo Island, offers a sanctuary for wildlife enthusiasts. The park is home to a diverse range of animals, including elephants, giraffes, chimpanzees, and over 400 bird species. Visitors can embark on nature walks, boat safaris, and bird-watching excursions to immerse themselves in the island's tranquil and biodiverse environment.

Preserving Mwanza's natural and cultural heritage is of great importance. Efforts are underway to promote sustainable tourism practices, protect the environment, and conserve the city's historical sites and landmarks. The Mwanza Museum showcases the region's rich history, including archaeological artifacts, cultural exhibits, and displays on the natural wonders of the Lake Zone.

In conclusion, Mwanza, the gateway to Lake Victoria, is a vibrant city that offers a captivating blend of natural beauty, cultural diversity, and historical significance. Its strategic location on the shores of Lake Victoria, its thriving markets, and its cultural festivals make it a compelling destination for visitors seeking to explore the wonders of Tanzania's Lake Zone. Mwanza's enduring charm lies in its ability to connect people to the majesty of Lake Victoria, the rich tapestry of its cultural heritage, and the warmth of its welcoming communities.

Arusha: A Hub for Safari Adventures and International Diplomacy

Nestled at the foothills of Mount Meru and in close proximity to the world-renowned Serengeti National Park and Mount Kilimanjaro, Arusha serves as a vibrant gateway to thrilling safari adventures and a hub for international diplomacy. This chapter explores the multifaceted nature of Arusha, from its natural wonders to its diplomatic significance, attracting visitors from around the globe.

Arusha, known as the "Geneva of Africa," is a city located in the northern part of Tanzania. Its strategic location near several national parks, including the Serengeti, Ngorongoro Conservation Area, Tarangire, and Lake Manyara, makes it a popular starting point for safari expeditions and wildlife experiences. The city's proximity to Mount Kilimanjaro, Africa's highest peak, further adds to its allure.

Safari enthusiasts flock to Arusha to embark on thrilling wildlife adventures in the nearby national parks. The Serengeti, known for its annual wildebeest migration, offers an unparalleled opportunity to witness one of nature's greatest spectacles. Visitors can observe majestic lions, graceful giraffes, and a myriad of other wildlife species in their natural habitats, creating unforgettable memories. The Ngorongoro Conservation Area, a UNESCO World Heritage Site, is another jewel in Arusha's crown. The area encompasses the stunning Ngorongoro Crater, a natural amphitheater teeming with diverse wildlife, including the endangered black rhino. Visitors can descend into the crater and marvel at the breathtaking landscapes and the rich ecosystem that exists within its confines. Arusha's natural beauty extends beyond its wildlife-rich parks. Mount Meru, the second-highest peak in Tanzania, offers thrilling trekking opportunities for outdoor enthusiasts. The mountain's slopes are adorned with lush forests, waterfalls, and an array of flora and fauna, creating a captivating environment for hikers and nature lovers.

Beyond its natural wonders, Arusha plays a significant role in international diplomacy. The city is home to the East African Community (EAC) headquarters, an intergovernmental organization that promotes regional integration and economic cooperation among its member states. The EAC serves as a platform for political dialogue, policy coordination, and economic development initiatives in East Africa.

Arusha's diplomatic importance is further enhanced by the presence of the International Criminal Tribunal for Rwanda (ICTR) and the Mechanism for International Criminal Tribunals (MICT). These institutions were established to address the atrocities committed during the 1994 Rwandan genocide and other conflicts in the region. The tribunals have played a crucial role in bringing justice and fostering reconciliation. The city of Arusha reflects its diplomatic significance through the presence of international organizations, diplomatic missions, and a diverse expatriate community. The multicultural atmosphere is evident in the city's restaurants, where a fusion of flavors from around the world can be savored.

Arusha's cultural heritage is also celebrated through various events and festivals. The Arusha Cultural Heritage Centre showcases the rich traditions, arts, and crafts of Tanzania's diverse ethnic groups. The center features exhibits on tribal cultures, traditional music, dance performances, and local artworks, providing a platform for cultural exchange and appreciation.

The vibrant Maasai community, known for their distinctive red attire and rich cultural heritage, also calls Arusha home. Visitors have the opportunity to learn about Maasai traditions, engage in cultural experiences, and support local community initiatives.

Arusha's position as a tourist hub has fueled the growth of its hospitality sector. The city offers a range of accommodation options, from luxury lodges to budget-friendly guesthouses, catering to the diverse needs and preferences of travelers. The bustling markets in Arusha, such as the Maasai Market, are popular spots for visitors to purchase souvenirs, traditional crafts, and locally made products. Efforts are being made to promote sustainable tourism practices and preserve Arusha's natural and cultural heritage. Initiatives focused on environmental conservation, community engagement, and responsible tourism are gaining momentum, ensuring that the region's natural wonders are protected for generations to come.

In conclusion, Arusha's unique blend of safari adventures and diplomatic significance make it a captivating destination in Tanzania. The city's proximity to world-renowned national parks and its role as a diplomatic center provide a diverse range of experiences for visitors. Whether exploring the awe-inspiring landscapes, engaging in cultural encounters, or participating in international forums, Arusha offers a gateway to both natural wonders and global diplomacy.

Dodoma: The Political Heart of Tanzania

Dodoma, situated in the heart of Tanzania, serves as the political capital and administrative center of the country. This chapter explores the significance of Dodoma, its role in Tanzanian politics, its historical roots, and the ongoing development that is shaping its future.

Dodoma became the capital of Tanzania in 1974, replacing Dar es Salaam. The decision to move the capital was driven by a desire to decentralize power and promote balanced development across the country. Dodoma's central location, both geographically and symbolically, made it an ideal choice for the new political center.

Dodoma's political importance is evident through the presence of government institutions, ministries, and the parliament. The Tanzanian Parliament, known as Bunge, convenes in Dodoma, where legislators gather to debate and pass legislation that shapes the nation's governance and policies. The parliamentary sessions provide a platform for political discourse, democratic processes, and decision-making.

The city's administrative significance is further reinforced by the presence of government offices and ministries, which are responsible for the implementation and coordination of national policies and programs. Dodoma serves as a hub for the country's bureaucratic machinery, ensuring effective governance and administrative functions.

Dodoma's historical roots can be traced back to the Gogo people, who have inhabited the region for centuries. The Gogo people have a rich cultural heritage and have played a significant role in shaping the local traditions, customs, and social fabric of Dodoma. Today, their cultural practices and artifacts can be explored at the Gogo Museum in the city.

The architecture of Dodoma reflects its administrative role. The cityscape features government buildings, ministerial complexes, and official residences. The iconic Parliament House, with its distinctive dome, stands as a symbol of Tanzanian democracy and political representation.

Dodoma's development as the political capital has led to ongoing infrastructure projects and urban expansion. The city is experiencing significant growth, with new residential areas, commercial centers, and educational institutions being established to accommodate the increasing population and administrative needs.

The University of Dodoma, founded in 2007, has become a prominent educational institution in Tanzania. The university offers a range of academic programs, contributing to the intellectual and human resource development of the country. It serves as a center for research, knowledge creation, and educational opportunities.

Dodoma's central location within Tanzania provides strategic advantages for transportation and connectivity. The city is well-served by road and rail networks, making it accessible from various parts of the country. The ongoing construction of the Standard Gauge Railway, which will connect Dodoma to other major cities, is set to further enhance connectivity and facilitate economic growth.

Efforts are underway to transform Dodoma into a modern and sustainable city. Urban planning initiatives focus on creating a well-designed and livable urban environment, with provisions for green spaces, efficient transportation systems, and improved infrastructure. The goal is to create a city that meets the needs of its residents while preserving the natural beauty of the surrounding landscape.

Dodoma's role as the political heart of Tanzania extends beyond administrative functions. The city hosts national events, conferences, and diplomatic gatherings, serving as a platform for national and international engagement. It showcases Tanzania's commitment to democracy, good governance, and regional cooperation.

In conclusion, Dodoma stands as the political heart of Tanzania, embodying the country's aspirations for balanced development, democratic governance, and administrative efficiency. Its central location, historical roots, and ongoing development make it a city of significance and potential. Dodoma's transformation as the political capital reflects Tanzania's vision for a prosperous and inclusive future, driven by the spirit of national unity and progress.

Mount Kilimanjaro: Conquering Africa's Highest Peak

Mount Kilimanjaro, the majestic snow-capped peak that soars above the African plains, holds a special place as the continent's highest mountain. This chapter explores the allure of Mount Kilimanjaro, its unique geographical features, the challenges and rewards of climbing it, and the significance it holds for those who undertake the journey.

Mount Kilimanjaro is located in northeastern Tanzania, near the border with Kenya. It is part of the Kilimanjaro National Park, a UNESCO World Heritage Site that encompasses the mountain and its surrounding ecosystems. The mountain stands tall at an elevation of 5,895 meters (19,341 feet), making it the highest free-standing mountain in the world.

One of the remarkable aspects of Mount Kilimanjaro is its unique ecosystem and diverse climatic zones. The mountain features five distinct ecological zones: the cultivated lower slopes, the lush rainforest, the heath and moorland, the alpine desert, and the arctic summit. Each zone presents its own distinct flora, fauna, and climatic conditions, offering climbers a truly extraordinary experience.

The ascent of Mount Kilimanjaro presents both physical and mental challenges. Climbers face altitude-related risks, extreme weather conditions, and the demands of trekking for multiple days. It is essential to acclimatize to the increasing altitude and follow a gradual ascent plan to minimize the risks of altitude sickness.

There are several popular routes to reach the summit of Mount Kilimanjaro, each offering a unique experience and varying levels of difficulty. The Machame Route, also known as the "Whiskey Route," is a challenging and scenic option that traverses diverse landscapes. The Marangu Route, often called the "Coca-Cola Route," is the most well-established and frequented route, providing comfortable hut accommodation along the way.

The Lemosho and Rongai routes offer more remote and less crowded experiences, with breathtaking vistas and wildlife encounters. The Northern Circuit Route, the newest and longest route, provides a panoramic traverse around the mountain, offering stunning views and the highest success rates.

Climbing Mount Kilimanjaro requires careful planning and preparation. It is recommended to engage the services of experienced guides and porters who are familiar with the mountain and its challenges. These guides play a crucial role in ensuring safety, providing guidance, and sharing their knowledge of the mountain's natural and cultural significance.

Reaching the summit of Mount Kilimanjaro, known as Uhuru Peak, is a momentous achievement and a source of immense pride for climbers. The feeling of standing atop the "Roof of Africa" and witnessing the breathtaking sunrise over the vast plains below is an unforgettable experience. The panoramic views of the surrounding landscape, including the distant Mount Meru and the sprawling Tanzanian savannah, create a sense of awe and wonder.

Mount Kilimanjaro's significance extends beyond the physical feat of conquering its summit. It holds cultural and spiritual importance for the Chagga people, who have lived in the foothills of the mountain for centuries. The Chagga regard Kilimanjaro as a sacred place, believing it to be the abode of their gods. Various rituals and ceremonies are performed to honor the mountain and seek blessings for a successful climb.

The allure of Mount Kilimanjaro transcends borders, attracting climbers from all corners of the globe. Its accessibility and diverse routes make it a popular choice for adventurers seeking to test their limits and experience the wonders of Africa's natural beauty. Climbing Kilimanjaro is not only a personal achievement but also an opportunity to connect with nature, challenge oneself, and forge lifelong memories.

Efforts are underway to preserve and protect Mount Kilimanjaro's fragile ecosystems and cultural heritage. Sustainable tourism practices, environmental conservation initiatives, and responsible trekking guidelines are in place to ensure the mountain's long-term sustainability and minimize the impact of human activity.

In conclusion, Mount Kilimanjaro stands as a monumental symbol of adventure, perseverance, and natural grandeur. Its towering presence, breathtaking landscapes, and cultural significance make it a beacon for those seeking to conquer Africa's highest peak. Climbing Kilimanjaro is a transformative journey that tests the body, challenges the mind, and rewards the spirit with awe-inspiring vistas and a profound sense of accomplishment.

Ruins of Kilwa Kisiwani and Songo Mnara: UNESCO World Heritage Sites

The ruins of Kilwa Kisiwani and Songo Mnara stand as testament to the rich historical and architectural heritage of the East African coast. These UNESCO World Heritage Sites offer a glimpse into the thriving trading cities that once flourished along the Swahili Coast. This chapter delves into the captivating history of Kilwa Kisiwani and Songo Mnara, their architectural wonders, and their significance in preserving the cultural legacy of the region.

Kilwa Kisiwani and Songo Mnara are located off the southern coast of Tanzania, in the Indian Ocean. These ancient trading ports were once powerful city-states and key players in the maritime trade network that connected Africa, Arabia, India, and China. The strategic location of these cities allowed them to control the trade of gold, ivory, spices, and other valuable commodities.

Kilwa Kisiwani, the larger of the two sites, was inhabited from the 9th to the 19th century CE and reached its peak during the 13th to 15th centuries. The city-state of Kilwa was renowned for its wealth, prosperity, and architectural achievements. It served as a major center of Islamic culture, attracting traders, scholars, and travelers from diverse backgrounds.

The ruins of Kilwa Kisiwani bear witness to the grandeur of its past. The Great Mosque, also known as the Friday Mosque, stands as an impressive architectural marvel. Built in the 13th century, it is one of the oldest mosques in East Africa and showcases the influence of Swahili, Persian, and

Arab architectural styles. The mosque's intricate coral stone carvings and ornate mihrab (prayer niche) are testaments to the skill and craftsmanship of the period.

The Palace of Husuni Kubwa, a magnificent structure that once housed the Kilwa Sultan, highlights the city's opulence and political power. The palace's imposing walls, courtyards, and underground chambers provide insights into the social and administrative functions of the time. The archaeological remains also reveal evidence of trade networks, including imported Chinese ceramics and Persian pottery fragments.

Songo Mnara, located on an adjacent island, was another important Swahili trading settlement. It flourished from the 14th to the 16th century before being abandoned. The ruins of Songo Mnara offer a glimpse into the city's layout, with its complex system of streets, public squares, and residential areas. The remains of coral stone houses, tombs, and defensive structures reflect the architectural ingenuity of the period.

Both Kilwa Kisiwani and Songo Mnara were recognized as UNESCO World Heritage Sites in 1981. These sites are not only remarkable for their historical and architectural significance but also for their contribution to our understanding of the Swahili civilization and its connections to the wider Indian Ocean world. They provide valuable insights into the cultural exchange, economic prowess, and urban planning of the time.

Preserving and safeguarding these sites is of utmost importance. Conservation efforts focus on maintaining the integrity of the ruins, protecting them from environmental degradation, and promoting sustainable tourism practices.

Local communities are actively involved in the preservation and management of the sites, ensuring their cultural and economic value is upheld for future generations.

Visiting the ruins of Kilwa Kisiwani and Songo Mnara is a captivating journey into the past. Exploring the archaeological sites, walking through the remnants of once-thriving cities, and marveling at the architectural achievements offers a unique opportunity to immerse oneself in the rich history and cultural heritage of the Swahili Coast.

In conclusion, the ruins of Kilwa Kisiwani and Songo Mnara stand as UNESCO World Heritage Sites, preserving the architectural wonders and historical significance of the Swahili civilization. These sites provide a window into the prosperous trading cities that once thrived along the East African coast. The ruins are a testament to the cultural exchange, economic prowess, and architectural ingenuity of the period, reminding us of the vibrant past and diverse heritage of the region.

Tanzanian Cuisine: A Fusion of Local and Global Flavors

Tanzanian cuisine reflects the diverse cultural influences and abundant natural resources of the country, resulting in a delightful fusion of local and global flavors. This chapter explores the rich culinary heritage of Tanzania, from traditional dishes to modern gastronomic trends, showcasing the vibrant tapestry of flavors that make up the country's diverse culinary landscape.

At the heart of Tanzanian cuisine is the use of fresh, locally sourced ingredients. With its fertile lands, coastal waters, and lush tropical climate, Tanzania boasts a bountiful array of fruits, vegetables, grains, spices, and seafood. The culinary traditions of various ethnic groups, such as the Swahili, Chagga, Sukuma, and Maasai, contribute to the diverse flavors and cooking techniques found throughout the country.

One iconic dish that represents Tanzanian cuisine is Ugali. Made from maize flour (cornmeal), it is a staple food in Tanzania and many other East African countries. Ugali has a thick porridge-like consistency and is often served alongside stews, curries, or grilled meat. It provides a hearty base to soak up the flavors of other dishes.

Tanzanian cuisine also embraces the abundant seafood available along its coastal regions. The Swahili influence is evident in dishes such as Coconut Fish Curry, where fresh fish is cooked in a flavorful coconut milk-based sauce, infused with aromatic spices like turmeric, cardamom, and cloves. Prawns, lobsters, and octopus are also popular choices, often prepared with a blend of spices and served with rice or chapati (flatbread).

The aromatic blend of spices is a hallmark of Tanzanian cuisine. The use of spices such as cinnamon, cloves, cumin, coriander, and ginger adds depth and complexity to dishes. Pilau, a fragrant rice dish, exemplifies this with its mix of spices, meat (usually chicken or beef), and vegetables. The dish is cooked slowly, allowing the flavors to meld together, creating a comforting and aromatic meal.

Meat lovers will delight in the variety of grilled and roasted meats that Tanzania has to offer. Nyama Choma, meaning "roasted meat" in Swahili, is a popular dish often enjoyed in social gatherings. It typically consists of skewered and grilled meat, such as beef, chicken, or goat, seasoned with a blend of spices and served with a side of fresh salad or chutney.

For those seeking vegetarian options, Tanzania's cuisine has much to offer. The use of legumes, such as lentils, chickpeas, and beans, is widespread. Dishes like Maharagwe, a flavorful coconut and kidney bean stew, or Ndizi Nyama, a banana and vegetable curry, provide a satisfying and nutritious alternative.

Tanzanian street food is an integral part of the culinary experience, offering a delightful range of flavors and textures. In bustling markets and roadside stalls, one can find popular snacks like Samosas (deep-fried pastries filled with savory fillings), Mishkaki (grilled skewered meat), and Mandazi (sweet fried doughnuts). These affordable and flavorful treats showcase the vibrant street food culture and the creativity of Tanzanian cuisine.

In recent years, Tanzanian cuisine has seen a fusion of traditional flavors with international influences. Modern restaurants and chefs are incorporating global culinary techniques and ingredients, creating innovative dishes that showcase the country's rich food culture in a contemporary context. This blending of local and global flavors is exemplified in dishes like Tanzanian-style pizza, which incorporates local spices and ingredients into the familiar Italian dish.

To accompany the diverse array of dishes, Tanzania offers a range of refreshing beverages. Tropical fruits such as mango, pineapple, and passionfruit are transformed into fresh juices, smoothies, and cocktails. The national beer, Kilimanjaro, is a popular choice, along with other locally brewed beers and traditional beverages like Maasai honey wine or coconut palm wine.

Tanzanian cuisine celebrates food as a social and cultural experience. Sharing meals with family and friends, whether at home or in local eateries, is an important part of Tanzanian culture. The warmth and hospitality of the Tanzanian people are often reflected in the generous portions and flavorsome dishes that are shared with guests.

In conclusion, Tanzanian cuisine is a vibrant fusion of local traditions and global influences. The country's rich cultural diversity, abundance of fresh ingredients, and flavorful spices create a culinary tapestry that entices and delights the senses. From traditional dishes to modern gastronomic innovations, Tanzania's cuisine is a testament to the country's culinary heritage and its ability to adapt and evolve with the changing times.

Conclusion

The history of Tanzania is a captivating tale of ancient civilizations, colonial encounters, and a quest for independence. From the prehistoric origins of humanity to the rise of powerful trading cities along the Swahili Coast, Tanzania's past is a mosaic of diverse cultures, struggles, and triumphs.

Throughout this book, we have explored the rich tapestry of Tanzania's history, delving into the ancient footsteps that shaped the land, the cultural exchanges that occurred along the Indian Ocean, and the moments of colonialism and resistance that defined the nation's path to independence.

We traced the emergence of powerful kingdoms and empires such as the Shamba Kingdom and the Maravi Federation, witnessing their influence and impact on the region. We marveled at the architectural wonders of Kilwa Kisiwani and the Omani influence that shaped Zanzibar. We examined the struggles against colonial rule, from German East Africa to the liberation movements that eventually led to Tanganyika's independence.

The birth of the United Republic of Tanzania marked a turning point, bringing together Tanganyika and Zanzibar under a unified vision of national unity, progress, and social justice. The leadership of Julius Nyerere, with his principles of Ujamaa and commitment to equality, left an indelible mark on the nation's identity and development.

We also explored the natural treasures of Tanzania, from the vast savannahs of the Serengeti to the unparalleled beauty of Mount Kilimanjaro. The wildlife conservation efforts and the preservation of UNESCO World Heritage Sites such as the ruins of Kilwa Kisiwani and Songo Mnara ensure that Tanzania's natural and cultural heritage is safeguarded for generations to come.

Tanzanian cuisine, with its fusion of local and global flavors, offers a delectable journey through the country's culinary traditions. From traditional dishes rooted in local ingredients and cooking techniques to the emergence of modern gastronomy, Tanzanian cuisine reflects the diversity and richness of the nation's cultural tapestry.

As we conclude this exploration of Tanzania's history, it is important to acknowledge that this book only scratches the surface of the nation's depth and complexity. Tanzania continues to evolve and shape its future, facing both challenges and opportunities.

The spirit of Tanzanian resilience, unity, and commitment to progress remains strong. The nation's vibrant cities, such as Dar es Salaam, Stone Town, and Dodoma, stand as symbols of growth and transformation. They reflect the ongoing development, urban planning, and commitment to sustainable practices that shape the nation's future.

Tanzania's journey is not without its challenges. Poverty, healthcare disparities, and environmental concerns require ongoing attention and concerted efforts. However, the nation's rich history, cultural heritage, and natural wonders provide a strong foundation upon which to build a brighter future.

As we close this book, let us appreciate the remarkable journey we have taken through the history, culture, and natural treasures of Tanzania. It is a land of ancient footprints, majestic landscapes, and a resilient people who continue to shape their destiny.

May this exploration inspire further curiosity, appreciation, and understanding of Tanzania's rich tapestry. Let us celebrate the legacy of the past and embrace the possibilities of the future as Tanzania continues to write its own story of progress, unity, and prosperity.

Dear Reader,

Thank you for embarking on this journey through the captivating history, cultural heritage, and natural wonders of Tanzania. It has been a pleasure to share this exploration with you, and I sincerely hope that you have found this book informative and engaging.

Your support and interest in the topics covered in this book are greatly appreciated. As a writer, there is nothing more rewarding than knowing that my words have resonated with readers like yourself. Your time and attention are valuable, and I am grateful for the opportunity to have been a part of your reading experience.

If you have enjoyed this book and found it insightful, I kindly request that you consider leaving a positive review. Your feedback not only encourages and motivates me as a writer but also helps other potential readers discover the value and quality of this book.

Printed in Great Britain
by Amazon